THE
SHAAR
PRESS

THE JUDAICA IMPRINT
FOR THOUGHTFUL PEOPLE

A
SHAAR
PRESS
PUBLICATION

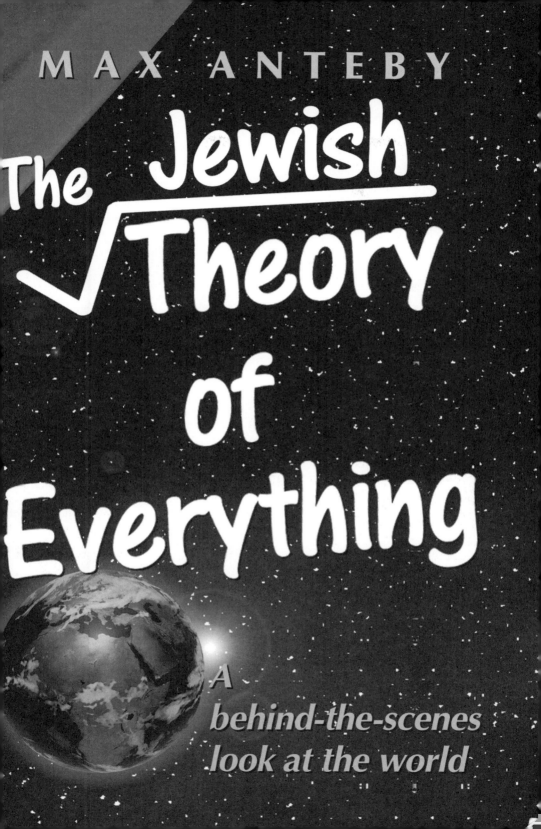

MAX ANTEBY

The $\sqrt{\dfrac{\text{Jewish}}{\text{Theory}}}$ of Everything

A behind-the-scenes look at the world

Published by **SHAAR PRESS**
Distributed by MESORAH PUBLICATIONS, LTD.
4401 Second Avenue / Brooklyn, N.Y 11232 / (718) 921-9000

Distributed in Israel by SIFRIATI / A. GITLER
6 Hayarkon Street / Bnei Brak 51127

Distributed in Europe by LEHMANNS
Unit E, Viking Industrial Park, Rolling Mill Road / Jarrow, Tyne and Wear, NE32 3DP/ England

Distributed in Australia and New Zealand by GOLDS WORLD OF JUDAICA
3-13 William Street / Balaclava, Melbourne 3183 / Victoria Australia

Distributed in South Africa by KOLLEL BOOKSHOP
Shop 8A Norwood Hypermarket / Norwood 2196, Johannesburg, South Africa

ISBN: 1-57819-578-0 Hard Cover
ISBN: 1-57819-579-9 Paperback

Printed in the United States of America by Noble Book Press
Custom bound by Sefercraft, Inc. / 4401 Second Avenue / Brooklyn N.Y. 11232

*"To make known
to mankind
His mighty acts..."*
Psalms 145:12

*This book is dedicated
to those
who have devoted
their lives
to attaining this goal.*

CONTENTS

How Big a Bang?

One of a Kind

Body and Soul

The Next Step

PREFACE

This is a book about God. Many people are familiar with the concept of an All-Powerful, All-Knowing Creator of the Universe. Unfortunately, many other people believe that after God finished the job of Creation (whatever that entailed), He went on the world's longest sabbatical. They feel that not only isn't He a personal God, He doesn't even know that we exist.

The goal of this book is to show that God not only knows that we exist and, indeed, knows every intimate detail about each one of us, but more importantly, God wants us to get to know about His existence, as much as that is possible. And, the more we get to know about Him, the happier, more pleasurable life we can lead.

The Jewish Theory of Everything has been written for the vast number of Jews who have little background in Jewish philosophy and practices as well as for those who have lived a lifetime of Torah observance. As such, I have intentionally not used any quotations from the Bible or Scriptures (except one) nor circular statements like, "We see that God created the world because it says in the Bible 'In the beginning God created the heavens and the earth.'" Rather, using everyday, real life examples I try to show that the phenomena of life could not possibly exist without there being a God who takes an interest in each one of us. It is my hope that after rationally considering each chapter, the reader will come to the same conclusion.

This book is based in large part on the classic work of Jewish philosophy called *The Duties of the Heart*. Written in the 12th century by Rabbeinu Bachya ibn Paquda, his chapter "Gates of Examination" (*Sha'ar HaBechinah*) details many of the ways that God relates to mankind in this world. I have also utilized an extensive list of standard scientific sources, most of which are taught on a high school or college level.

The impetus behind writing this book was my desire to express a personal thank you to one of the great men of this generation, my teacher, the late RABBI AVIGDOR MILLER, זצ"ל (in Hebrew, "*zichrono tzaddik l'vrachah*," of blessed memory). More than anyone else in our time, he was a living example of the precepts outlined in *Sha'ar HaBechinah*. For over 60 years, he taught these ideas to thousands of students around the world through his books, lectures and tapes. For those who were fortunate enough to have learned from him, they will find many familiar stories and phrases in the following pages. With his passing, we lost a giant of Torah and a true teacher of wisdom.

It is most appropriate that I thank my family for giving me the time and space to work on this project and for acting as my sounding board for all of the jokes. First, I would like to thank all of my daughters – Ruth, Grace, Karen, Elana, Rebecca and Sarah – for giving meaning to my life. I would particularly like to thank my daughter Elana for typing several chapters of the manuscript and to my sons-in-law for their enthusiastic encouragement. I would also like to thank my parents for teaching me the fine art of story-telling and imbuing me with a sense of humor. To all of my teachers I owe a debt of gratitude for opening my eyes to the wonders of the world and to the beauty and joy of the Jewish faith.

I am forever grateful to the staff of Shaar Press who graciously worked with me to present my work to the public. Additionaly, I would like to thank CHARLOTTE FRIEDLAND for her careful and caring editing of my manuscript and to ELI KROEN for his cover design.

Thank you also to ZVI, JERRY and MICHAEL for creating an office environment that is conducive to hard work, Torah study and creativity.

Finally, special thanks to my wife, Susan, for always keeping the midnight oil burning. None of my accomplishments in life would be possible without her.

Sit back, enjoy the ride and more importantly, enjoy life.

Max Anteby
Brooklyn, New York

What's It All About?

CLOSE ENCOUNTERS

On April 12, 1961, a young Russian cosmonaut stepped in front of the cameras, as he was about to board his spacecraft, Vostok 1, for what was going to be man's first voyage into outer space. Yuri Gagarin announced, "Now I go to meet nature face to face in an unprecedented encounter."

For the next several hours, Gagarin encountered nature in a way that no man had done before, far beyond the reaches of the clouds, to a place bordering on the infinite. He had an awesome responsibility to chronicle for mankind what existed outside the Earth's realm and man's control.

Upon his return to earth he remarked, "Now I know that God does not exist, because I was there and I didn't see him."

but that's the pt.! G-d stays hidden so we have the ability to search

Less than one year later, John H. Glenn entered his spacecraft, Freedom 7, in America's attempt to beat the Russians in the race to space. He brought a Bible along with him. As he peered through the small window of his capsule, he looked out on the enormity of the universe and on the delicate fragility of our own Earth. He felt the presence of the "Hand of Almighty God" as he recited from the first chapter of Genesis.

Two men, with identical experiences, unprejudiced by anything that had gone before them. One saw God, the other denied His existence. it's simply a matter of perspective

In reality, only one of them can be right because there can be only one answer to the question: Does God exist?

THE
FIRST STEP

When you speak to someone about God, he'll usually tell you, "Yeah, I sort of know there's a God. Maybe He created the world, maybe He's still involved in the world, maybe He's not. I never really thought about it – I'm much too busy! I work 40 to 50 hours a week, I car pool three times a week, I go to the gym at night, on Tuesdays there's the Board meeting at my kid's school. On Saturdays, sometimes I go to synagogue. Sunday – that's my time. When do I have a chance to think about God?"

That's the first reason why most people fail to recognize that there's a God – they're so involved in worldly pursuits and, thank God, everything is going so well, who has time to think about Him?

There's also a second reason. Growing up in America, we have access to unlimited bounty. Even a lower middle income family living in America today has it better than the richest of kings who lived only 500 years ago – just by virtue of having indoor plumbing and air conditioners!

As children, we get toys, food, clothing, presents, vacations, a roof over our heads and our own bedrooms. As we mature, we believe that these are all essential parts of our being, there to satisfy our human instincts for food, shelter and clothing. Not that we feel we deserve it for any particular merit on our part, but rather we fail to consider that there might be a Creator Who is giving all of this to us: it all seems simply natural.

Another reason people might not see a benevolent, loving God is that they focus on the problems and mishaps of everyday life. They conclude that it's impossible for God to exist: a loving God would never treat me like this! They get angry any time something bad happens and if something good ever happens, they consider it a fluke.

They are like a group of blind people who've been admitted to a residence that's been specifically designed and furnished with everything they need for their comfort. Everything has been put in the right places, ergonomically suited for their ease of use. There's even a full staff of doctors and nurses equipped with medicines and treatments to help their sightless condition improve.

However, as the days go by, they ignore the advice of the doctors and they don't follow their directions. They wander about aimlessly, miserable because of their blindness, stumbling over all of the articles that were left there for their benefit. They fall down, bruise themselves, stub their toes and worse. So, naturally, they start complaining about the proprietor and the builder and the doctors. They accuse the manager of failing in his responsibility and they're convinced that his sole aim was not to bestow kindness, but rather to cause them pain and agony.

And of course, there's always that fourth type of person who says, "There is no God. Everything is an accident. Whatever good happens to me is because I've earned it – I did it all myself."

So whether you've been preoccupied, oblivious, resentful or non-believing up until this point, let's spend the next few pages together examining the nature of this Being we call God and test the theory that He is behind Everything.

There are three approaches we could take:

The "Fire and Brimstone Approach" – which went over a lot better during the days of the prophets, or; G-d used to send prophecies of destruction to scare ppl. to do His will

The "Do It Because Your Grandfather Did It Approach" – which worked for many generations, but no longer appeals to today's mindset, or; G-d does J'lnc → see G-d and I don't need to question

The "Rational Approach" – which makes sense? (You can read that with or without the question mark.) our society needs rational, logical answers

I have chosen to use a rational, yet light-hearted, approach to this very serious subject to show that learning about God can be an enjoyable experience and that it does not require a "leap of faith."

While we are examining the phenomena of the universe and nature, the origin of life, and the spiritual side of man's being, we will be noting that they all have one thing in common – they all work towards the benefit of mankind.

Why should that be so? What is so unique about us that we should be the focal point of all existence?

In the final analysis, we will see that there is a kind, loving Father of all humanity – God, who created man in order to have someone upon whom to shower His goodness. By definition, God is the Source of all goodness.

In addition, God created us as beings capable of understanding all of the good that is being bestowed upon us. We just have to be willing to see it. The more we recognize the Hand of God in all the things around us, the more we appreciate what He does for us, the closer we will naturally feel to Him, just as a child feels towards his parents. When we've accomplished that, we are then prepared to get the maximum amount of pleasure out of everything this world has to offer. we have the ability to see goodness and it's for our benefit

The first step is the key, and might be the hardest: to recognize that there is a God who is the Creator of the Universe.

But don't just take my word for it. Read on thoughtfully and then decide: Is this world and all existence an accident, or must it be a planned and purposeful kindness from our Creator?

Let's begin to take that first step in looking for the Hand of God in Everything, and then see which concept makes more sense.

Darwin –
Survival
of a
Theory

PLANE TALK

An elderly New York rabbi needed to fly to Atlanta to deliver a sermon. As he was getting on in age, he decided to take his son along with him. They arrived at Kennedy Airport only to find that the flight was fully booked and that their seats were 18 rows apart. They decided that since the flight is usually less bumpy in the front of the plane, the rabbi would sit up front and the 40-year-old son would sit in the back.

As luck would have it, sitting to the left of the rabbi was a priest of about the same age and, on his right, a businessman who took one look at his companions and busied himself with his laptop.

After all of the passengers had settled in, the son came to check on his father.

"Abba, would you like a pillow for your head?"

"No, thank you, I'm going to try and do a little reading. But maybe you can get me a blanket."

The son asked one of the flight attendants for a blanket, which she found in one of the overhead bins, and he gave it to his father.

About half an hour into the flight, the pilot turned off the "Fasten Seat Belts" sign. The son immediately got up again and checked on his father.

"Abba, is everything all right?"

"Yes, thank you Reuven."

"Can I get you anything?"

"No, no I'm fine."

Reuven motioned to the priest who was sitting in the aisle seat, "Excuse me, sorry to disturb you."

The priest nodded a polite hello, and Reuven returned to his seat. The short flight from New York to Atlanta offered what the airlines considered an in-flight snack consisting of yogurt, a muffin, a banana and a small package of hard cheese. The rabbi and his son had ordered a kosher meal, which consisted of two slices of still-frozen pastrami, a soggy roll and a smear of mustard. (No one is exactly sure why airlines think that Jewish people eat pastrami for breakfast, but that's what they served).

After the stewardess had delivered their kosher meals, Reuven got up from his seat for a third time, filled a plastic cup with some water from the kitchenette sink and brought it over to his father with a small basin so that he could do the Jewish ritual washing of his hands before eating bread. The rabbi took the cup, washed his hands and said the traditional blessings.

After Reuven had gone back to his seat, the priest remarked, "Your son is certainly very caring."

"Thank you," the rabbi replied.

"I wish I could see more of that type of behavior from the children in my parish."

"Oh, you mean they don't have such respect for their parents?"

"They used to, especially when I was growing up, but not today's generation. They're more independent. They don't seem to have that feeling of respect for their elders. I don't know why that is," sighed the priest, "probably just a sign of the times."

"May I offer you a possible explanation?"

"Sure, I'd love to hear it."

At this point, the priest turned slightly toward the rabbi to better hear what he had to say. The businessman paused for a moment, hoping to hear something that might satisfy his own curiosity.

"We're both familiar with the Bible, aren't we?"

"Certainly, it's required reading in order to get one of these," the priest joked as he touched his white collar.

"Then let's look at the story of creation."

"Yes, the first chapter of Genesis. The parable of how God created the world in six days."

"Exactly the point. You see, we Jews believe literally that mankind, beginning with Adam, was created in the image of God. All of us have a part of God inside of us, a soul. The Bible also tells us about our forefathers, Abraham, Isaac, and Jacob, and how God spoke to each of them."

"Yes, I've read those stories many times."

"Of course. And you've also read about Moses, our greatest prophet. The Bible tells us that God spoke to Moses and the entire Jewish nation at Mount Sinai when He gave them the Ten Commandments."

"Yes, please continue."

"We Jews trace our heritage back to the original tribes of Israel. We have Cohanim with us today who are direct descendents of Aaron, the first high priest. Other Jews come from the tribe of Levi, those who served in the Holy Temples. We take great pride in our heritage."

"Yes, I'm aware of that. But that doesn't seem to answer my question about respecting your elders."

"Ah, my dear friend, but it does. You see, we believe that the further back you go, the closer you are to the holy generations of the nation of Israel – the prophets, the kings, the twelve tribes, and our forefathers. The older you are, the closer you are to someone who stood at the foot of Mount Sinai and saw God.

"Now if I understand correctly, the major philosophy of the Western world is that you are not descended from great people, but rather, according to Darwin, that you descended from a common ancestor of the apes. Therefore the further back you go, the closer you get to being like a monkey. And why should a monkey get any respect?"

The priest was momentarily silent. The businessman started getting a little bit edgy.

The rabbi continued. "I would suspect that the thinking of the younger generation is that the further away you get from the early generations, the more you've progressed to being fully human! So rather than sons respecting parents, the parents should respect the sons. Don't you see that this can only lead to the breakdown of the family and society?"

At this point, the businessman could contain himself no longer. "Excuse me rabbi, but I've been listening to the two of you and there's no way I can accept what you're saying! It goes against everything we learned in school. How do you explain Darwin? He's got fossils; he's got real proof. You could go to any museum and see them. Monkeys, apes, Neanderthal skeletons, and modern man, they're all there. What Darwin said makes perfect sense. It's *science*."

"Yes," the rabbi mused, "and scientists used to believe that the Earth was flat – until they took a broader perspective and disproved their own theory."

"Well, they're never going to disprove this one. If they do, I'll be a monkey's uncle!"

The rabbi and priest glanced at each other.

"Excuse me, fine sir," the priest replied, "I think you have that backwards."

TWO DEFINITIONS

Definition Number 1

Science – the systematic observation of the phenomena of nature and the universe to develop laws and principles based on those facts.

When I was nine years old, I got my first chemistry set. It contained over 60 different chemicals with test tubes, tin measuring spoons and two boxes of litmus paper. None of the chemicals were strong enough to blow up the house, but when I mixed two of the powders together and the water turned bright red, wow! That was exciting. And no matter how many times I did the experiment, I always got the same result. That's science.

Definition Number 2

Philosophy – a set of opinions about life and the world such as the belief in or denial of the existence of God.

Ten years later when I entered college, I had some professors who spoke about the benefits of capitalism over communism, immorality over Puritanism and the rights of the individual within a collective society. That's philosophy.

I had another professor in Advanced Biology who spoke about Darwin's theory of the evolution of man. He had charts and pictures all over the lab that looked like trees with different animals attached to them. He spoke of the fossil records showing the gradual changes within each organism over millions of generations that indicated that the higher forms of life developed from the simpler organisms that preceded them.

When asked where these fossils were that showed the transitional changes, he said that we were still looking for them. He later remarked that we've been looking for them for the last 200 years.

When pressed further, he said that no one had actually observed one species evolve into another, neither millions of years ago nor today. Is it possible, then, that Darwin's theories may not be a true science but just wishful thinking?

The late Professor Stephen J. Gould was the co-author of the most currently accepted theory of evolution called "Punctuated Equilibrium." His theory basically states that new life forms appeared suddenly in the fossil record with no transitional stages preceding them. (Ahem, as though they were just "created" out of thin air, we may wonder.)

Professor Gould had this to say about Darwin's particular brand of science:

"It was not inductive science, it was not based on observation, but it was a mere philosophy."

Maybe we should read Definition Number 2 again:

Philosophy – a set of opinions about life and the world such as the belief in or denial of the existence of God.

CLEAN-UP TIME

Many times when someone wants to make a point about evolution they'll "set you up" with two questions. The first question is usually like one of these:

"If you found a watch in a desert, would you ever think that it just happened to come into being by itself?"

Or, "If you saw a ten-story building, would you assume that over a millennia of time the necessary components came together all by themselves and constructed a finely engineered multi-story building?"

And you usually answer them, no, of course not. Somebody was responsible for conceiving, designing, assembling and constructing each one.

The follow-up question then becomes: If you accept that there is a level of intelligence necessary to produce these complex items, why would you think that mankind, with all of its complexity of genes, DNA, emotions and abilities could have come into being by accident?

Now, you may have one of three answers to this question. Your Number One answer could be, "Because."

Number Two: (after thinking it out a little more) "Because that's what they taught us in high school."

And if you've ever heard the question before and you've considered your response for a while, answer Number Three could go something like this: "Most people understand that inanimate physical objects such as watches, buildings and planes have been made by craftsmen or builders. Since we see this happening all of the time, we have firsthand experience and we know that they didn't happen by themselves.

"However, when we see tadpoles grow into frogs, or caterpillars turn into butterflies, or fleas become pesticide resistant, it is possible to infer that, given enough time, a single-celled organism could evolve on its own into a more complex organism and ultimately into a fish, a reptile or a man."

Sounds reasonable to me.

So now let's use our reason and see if it's possible. Consider the following scene: It's Mother's Day and you've decided to invite your kids and grandchildren over for the day. You order in pizza for the grandchildren and you make a casserole and steamed vegetables for your children and their spouses.

After you finish lunch, you send the little ones off to play in the den so you can enjoy a quiet cup of coffee and some hot apple pie with the other "grownups."

At four o'clock, it's time for everyone to leave. You go into the den to say goodbye to the little darlings and it looks like a cyclone hit the place. Toys, pretzels, games, books and papers are everywhere. You left the room clean and organized, and it turned into chaos. And you know perfectly well why. Not because your son-in-law doesn't know how to bring up his kids, but because there was no one supervising.

So, you spend the next twenty minutes tapping your foot with your arms folded and a stern look on your face, explaining to them exactly where everything goes and how to use a Dust Buster.

Without knowing it, your grandchildren have just demonstrated an important scientific principle. It's known as the Second Law of Thermodynamics. It states that any " closed system" (kids playing in a house) that doesn't have "positive input" (someone watching) tends towards "entropy" (mess). However, once a degree of control is placed onto "the system," its natural tendency to become even more disorganized is reversed. Of course, the bigger the mess (chaos) the more organization (energy) required to return it to its original state (cosmos).

So now, let's take another look at your reasonable assumption of amoeba becoming human.

The theory of evolution requires that the simple become complex without any supervision or positive, intelligent input. The problem with this, according to science itself, is that this doesn't occur anywhere in the universe – not in the most remote galaxies, and not even in your own backyard. In fact, everywhere you look, there are a lot more ways for things to get more disorganized than there are ways for them to get better.

In other words, it's a lot easier to make a mess than it is to keep your den (or the universe) neat. Unless there is positive input and intelligence guiding the process, there has to be chaos.

Darwin says just the opposite. Over a span of millions of years, totally by accident, without any control, amoeba become fish, fish become reptiles or birds, they then become land creatures which eventually find their way through the evolutionary chain to become intelligent, complex human beings reading this book.

Cosmos from chaos, without energy. It's impossible. Science itself has proven it.

Order out of disorder, without effort. It just can't happen.

Ask your housekeeper. She'll tell you.

A SURE BET

What would you do if you went to the race-track and somebody came over to you and gave you a hot tip? He says horse number 32 is a sure bet to win in the next race. You figure it's only $2.00, what could you lose? You walk over to the betting window and there's another stranger betting on a different horse. You ask him, "What about horse 32?" He answers, "Nah, I don't know. I just don't think he's gonna win."

Would you place the bet? A moment ago it was just $2.00. Now, hey, it's *my* $2.00 and I'm not going to throw it away on a bum lead.

We see this happen in real life all of the time. A person will tell you about something that he feels very strongly about, and then some time later you find him changing his mind. Let's look at one particular example.

Charles Darwin proposed a theory 150 years ago. It stated that man evolved from lower life forms. He wrote his magnum opus called *On the Origin of Species by Means of Natural Selection* which, interestingly enough, never addresses the question of how life "originated." Nevertheless, Darwin put forth what he was sure was a cogent, verifiable recounting of how man evolved. And then, halfway through, he turns skeptical. He writes:

A crowd of difficulties occur. Some of them are so serious that to this day, I can hardly reflect on them without being in some degree staggered.

One of the chief objections which might be justly waged against the views maintained herein, one namely the distinctiveness of specific forms and their not being blended together by innumerable transitional links is a very obvious difficulty.

He's referring here not only to the missing links between monkeys and apes and mankind, but also the missing links between each series in the supposed chain from single-cell algae to all of the higher forms throughout the chain.

Darwin continues:

I can answer these questions and objections only on the supposition that the geological record is far more imperfect than most geologists believe. That the geological record is imperfect all will agree. But that it is imperfect to the degree required by this theory, few will be inclined to admit.

In other words, to prove the theory of evolution, Darwin and his followers would have had to find the transitional links between one species and another. To date, the fossil record has failed to provide any support for his theory. This fact has prompted the curator of the American Museum of Natural History, Mr. Niles Eldridge, to state, "The fossil record that we have been looking for in the past [150] years does not exist."

So if Darwin himself didn't believe his own theory, it is only natural to expect theologians to be even more skeptical.

Consider this comment from one of the great sages of the 20th century, Rabbi Avigdor Miller:

The most obvious refutation of the theory of evolution is the inescapable fact that in a world full of human beings there is not one sub-human or super-human either alive or in a fossil state. Where are the men with tails or hooves or wings, or any of the countless variations that could have developed?

The rate of probability for accidental development of even one of the most simple of man's components is against astronomically calculated odds.

The author is skeptical of his own theory. Perhaps there are others who do believe. Following are a few quotes for you to ponder:

"Natural selection may explain the *survival* of the fittest but it can never explain the *arrival* of the fittest." – Hugo DeVries (Professor of Botany at the University of Amsterdam, the originator of the Mutation Theory)

"It appears that the mathematical, the artistic and the musical faculty could not possibly have developed [in mankind] by means of natural selection." – A.R. Wallace (a contemporary of Darwin who wrote the famous *Wallace Paper* of 1855)

"The origin of birds is largely a matter of deduction. There is no fossil evidence of the stages through which the change from reptile to bird was achieved." – W. E. Swinton (author of *Biology and the Comparative Physiology of Birds*)

"The fossil record does not tell us how fish came into existence." – U. Lunham (Professor of Oceanography, University of Marseilles)

"I still think that to the unprejudiced, the fossil record of plants is in favor of special creation." – E. J. H. Corner (author of *Evolution in Contemporary Botanical Thought*)

"Nobody can explain how evolution operated but we will uphold it even if only as an act of faith." – D. H. Scott (quoted in *The History of Warfare of Science with Theology* by A.D. White)

"Though our faith in evolution stands unbroken, we have no acceptable account of the origin of the species." – Professor David Bateson (Manchester College, England)

"The statistical probability that organic structures and the precisely harmonized reactions that typify living organisms would be generated by accident is zero." – Dr. I. Prigogine (recipient of two Nobel Prizes in Chemistry)

"The evolutionary theory is itself one of the strangest phenomena of humanity. That in our time, a system destitute of any shadow of proof, supported only by vague analysis or figures of speech should be accepted, is surprisingly strange." – Sir J.W. Dawson (quoted in *The History of the Warfare of Science with Theology* by A.D. White)

And that, ladies and gentlemen, is what makes horse races.

KEEP YOUR EYE ON THE BALL

I don't want to bore you with all those "little" things about the human eye that everyone talks about: Like the fact that it is one million times faster than the fastest computers on the market today. (The eye processes one billion Million Images per Second [MIPS] compared to one thousand MIPS for a computer.) Or the fact that we have two totally different sets of vision, one for processing color and one at night for black and white. And I'm not going to tell you about how we have transparent cells in our eyeballs that allow light to pass through them. And I won't even mention how we can see through these cells, even though they have blood cells passing through them.

That's all child's play. I want to discuss the really heavy stuff.

Imagine it's one million years ago and these two prehistoric men are playing catch. Jake takes a rock and tosses it over to Pete. Pete goes to catch it and it lands on his head. Pete picks it up and throws it back to Jake. Jake stretches his arms out for it and it falls right between his hands. Jake picks up the rock again and throws it back to Pete, but it sails twenty feet over his head.

The dejected duo sits down on a nearby stump. Jake says mournfully, "Pete, how are we ever going to have a World Series if we can't even catch a rock?"

Pete thinks about it pensively and says, "You know what our problem is, Jake? We only have one eye in the center of our heads. We lack depth perception." (Neanderthal men spoke about this type of thing all the time.)

Pete continues, "You know what we have to do, Jake? We have to work on our genetic material to produce a second eye."

"A grand idea," exclaims Jake. (Jake never would have thought of it on his own.)

Think about it for a moment. If the theory of evolution is correct, from where did we get two eyes? At what point in the evolutionary cycle would we have gotten even *one* eye?

Maybe it was when all the fish were swimming at the bottom of the rivers and they got tangled up in the plant life that they decided they needed eyes. Or maybe it was after they became reptiles, and they kept walking off the sides of cliffs, that they understood that the only way to survive was to develop eyesight. So how did these unseeing clusters of cells know that there was such a thing as vision?

So maybe it was just an accident. That's it. It had to be an accident since evolution could never be working *towards* a goal because that would imply an outside director. Modern scientists don't approve of "directed development," because that smacks of Divine intervention.

deny that there is a purpose in the world

So, okay, it was an accident, a sudden mutation. But if it was an accident, how is it that they developed two, perfectly alike, synchronized, coordinated, yet complementary eyes? This happened to happen not only to fish and reptiles, but also to mammals and mollusks and insects and birds. And they all developed almost identically featured eyes with pupils that dilate, lenses that focus, muscles that move in coordination, tear ducts that lubricate, eyelids that protect, rods and cones that receive and process light and optic nerves that transmit these light signals to the brain. And they all developed from virtually the same gene location on the chromosome – which also had to have gotten there by accident in each of the species that evolutionists agree *did not* evolve one from the other.

It doesn't sound too likely that *all* of that could have happened, repeatedly, by itself, by accident. Then, perhaps, eyesight is just one of those great blessings bestowed on all creatures by the Creator of the world in order for them to survive. Animals need it to find food, birds need it for flight and mankind needs it to read yesterday's baseball scores.

He has left His fingerprints all over creation. We just have to keep our eyes on the ball in order to see them.

THE NERVE

My son-in-law is a genius. He was valedictorian of his high school, he graduated summa cum laude from college, he has a Masters degree in Business and he was smart enough to marry my daughter.

Recently, at a Friday night Shabbat meal, I asked him, " What's a synapse?"

He thought about it a moment and said, "That's when you fall asleep in *syn*-agogue on Yom Kippur."

I politely corrected him and told him, "In that case, it would be spelled with two 'n's."

A synapse, of course, is the space between two nerve endings in the human body. Our bodies are wired with thousands of miles of nerves connecting almost all of our thirty trillion cells to the brain. (Hair, for example, doesn't have nerves, but the roots do – that's why we feel it when we brush our hair but not when we cut it.)

Two questions! Why do we have these spaces and how did we get them?

Answer #1: Synapses are there to shield the brain from unwanted stimuli. How does that work?

Have you ever wondered how a newborn can fall asleep in a hospital nursery in the middle of 12 screaming babies?

Synapse.

Have you ever been on the floor of the New York Stock Exchange? Four hundred traders are shouting at each other, yet everybody can focus just on his own conversation. This "directional hearing" is part of the workings of the nervous system and synapse.

There are also some very important bodily reasons for them. After you swallow a spoonful of fresh corn flakes, do you ever feel them scratching all the way down your esophagus? Not usually. That's because of the types of nerve endings in your food pipe and the weaker connections they have with the brain. Each organ of the body is wired according to the necessity of feeling sensations in its particular area.

For example, I recently had a sinus infection and the doctor wanted to take a sinus culture. He cautioned me that I might feel a little tickle inside my sinuses when he took the culture. What he really meant was, "Try not to jump too high when I touch the back of your eyeballs with the probe."

I discovered that there are parts of the inside of my head that I never knew existed. How come I never felt sensations in them before, even when I breathed in cold winter air?

Synapse.

There's no question that they perform a very necessary function in allowing the body to focus and concentrate only on what's important to us.

Now here's the rub – how did we get them?

Answer #2: Well, according to the theory of evolution and the "survival of the fittest," you would have to say that early man –

Neanderthals and Cro-Magnons – didn't have synapses. They felt every sensation of the body including breathing, digesting and itchy clothing. (Perhaps that's why they always walked around hunched over, with a club in their hand like they're ready to hit somebody). Slowly but surely, after millions of generations, those who were sane enough to survive their nervous overload somehow learned to produce calmer children who had synapses. The rest of them without synapses probably just had nervous breakdowns and died off.

If, however, you believe in the creation of the world by a loving, caring, kind Creator, then there's no question as to why we have synapses or how we got them. The same way the body is protected from invasion of unseen bacteria and viruses by antibodies, the nervous system protects our most important organ, the brain, from outside influences that would take away our ability to operate at peak performance.

Accident of nature or planned kindness by the Original Manufacturer? Which makes more sense?

By the way, scientists still don't fully understand why husbands ignore their wives when they tell them to put their dirty laundry in the hamper.

Synapse, perhaps.

ONCE OVER LIGHTLY

(It is a normal day in Smalltown, USA; a day just like all the rest. Thomas Bogan walks into his favorite restaurant on his way to work. He is greeted by his usual waitress.)

Marge: Morning, Mr. Bogan.

Tom: Hi, Marge, how are you today?

Marge: Doin' fine. Is it still rainin' outside?

Tom: Yeah, it is. Don't you just love a rainy day, especially on the way into work?

Marge: My favorite kind o' day. What are ya' havin' today, the usual toasted bagel, cup o' coffee?

Tom: You know what, I'm a little hungry. How's about two eggs, once over lightly, and a little orange juice?

Marge: You got it.

(*Tom opens his newspaper and starts reading the front page. Politics, foreign news and the economy. Five minutes later, he finishes reading the whole first page and he notices that Marge hasn't come back with his order. He calls to one of the other waitresses.*)

Tom: Hey, Julie, have you seen Marge?
Julie: What's the matter, she didn't bring your order yet?
Tom: Not yet.
Julie: Just one sec, I'll get her for you.
Tom: Thanks.

(*Marge appears after a moment carrying Tom's glass of orange juice.*)

Marge: Sorry, about that, Mr. Bogan, the cook said he was havin' some problems with the eggs. It'll just be another minute.
Tom: No problem.

(*Tom opens up the paper to the editorials. Politics, foreign news and the economy. Another five minutes go by and suddenly Marge appears.*)

Marge: I'm really sorry, Mr. Bogan, but it's incredible.
Tom: Why, what's going on?
Marge: Gus has been trying to make you your eggs, but he can't get the shells to crack.
Tom: That's impossible. An eggshell can't be very thick.

(*Just then, a very agitated Gus comes in from the kitchen.*)

Gus: Sorry, Marge, but I never seen nothing like this before. It's unbelievable. Hi, Tom.
Tom: Hi, Gus.
Marge: What is?
Gus: They're all dead, all twelve of 'em.
Tom: Who's dead?

Gus: The chicks. I finally opened up all twelve eggs. I used the hammer and the ice pick. It's the freakiest thing I ever saw. It's like the mother hen tried to hatch 'em, but it didn't work. Those shells were too thick. Those poor chicks, they just...

Marge: Take it easy, Gus, it'll be all right.

Gus: I..I..I can't. I been doin' this all my life. Ever since I was a mess sergeant back in Korea. I been working with eggs, all kindsa eggs. I ain't never heard of an eggshell too thick for the chicks to come out.

Marge: Where'd you get them from?

Gus: We bought them down at Yazkor's farm. He was running some kind of special on them.

Marge: You mean old man Yazkor? He's been a little weird, ever since the '70's.

Tom: Maybe he nuked them.

Marge: You mean like they're some kind of mutation?

Gus: Sure, that would be the only way. The only problem is that sudden mutations would make them weaker in the long run, not stronger.

Marge: You sure? What about those Mutant Ninja Turtles? My kids tell me they're pretty strong.

Gus: Fairy tales, Marge. (*Putting on a pair of glasses, then folding his arms*) Scientists say that any type o' mutation o' the genes strong enough to change something like this is never good for the species. In fact, mutations are even less likely to be able to have offspring. Even if there was offspring, after a few generations the DNA safety mechanism would kick in an' the species would go back to its original state.

Tom: Wow, Gus, it sounds like you know an awful lot about this stuff.

Gus: Eggs is sorta my hobby.

Marge: So what you're saying is the way it is today is the way it always had to be.

Tom: I read about this recently. Microevolution happens all the time, but so far scientists haven't found any evidence of macroevolution.

Gus: You mean, like, one species evolving into another.

Tom: Right. I'm saying that the chicken had to get the eggshell right the first time.

Marge: What do you mean by "right," Mr. Bogan?

Gus: He means that the eggshell has to be thick enough to take the pressure of the hen laying the egg, but not too thick for the baby chick to peck its way out of it.

Marge: But that don't sound so hard.

Tom: There must be thousands of possible thicknesses that wouldn't work and only one that would.

Gus: Marge, look at it this way. Suppose that the first eggshells were too thin. Every time the egg came out, the chick would be nothing more than clear jelly and yellow goo. So how would the next generation ever be born?

Tom: Well, maybe it was just an accident, and only those hens that happened to produce the right thickness shell survived and all the others died off. You know, like, the survival of the fittest.

Gus: But that means that Mother Nature would've had to repeat that same accident millions of times.

Marge: Sure. And we're only talking about chickens. What about alligators? They lay eggs.

Tom: That's right. And birds.

Marge: And fish, and reptiles.

Gus: And ostriches. And each egg is exactly right for that species. And it always had to be, otherwise none of them would have survived.

Tom: Just like those twelve eggs in the kitchen.

Gus: You didn't have to remind me.

Marge: Gus, so let me get this straight. What you're saying is, it sort of had to be planned that way.

Tom: But who could have planned it?

Marge: Maybe there's this great Creator that designed the whole universe. An' He made everything run perfectly, just for us.

Tom: Marge, that's very deep.

Marge: Thanks, Mr. Bogan.

Tom: Please, call me Tom.

Marge: Okay. Tom.

Tom: What you're saying is, maybe nothing is an accident – that there's a God that plans everything for the good of mankind.

Marge: Am I sayin' that?

Tom: Yeah. Sorta.

(Tom and Marge stare at each other.)

Gus: *(After a moment)* I guess I'll be getting back to the kitchen. I got a pretty big mess to clean up. *(He leaves.)*

Marge: Well. What do you think, Tom?

Tom: *(Coming back to reality)* I think it's late. You better make it a toasted bagel and a cup of coffee to go.

Marge: Sure, Mr. Bogan.

(Tom neatly folds his newspaper as Marge heads back to the kitchen.)

The Natural Look

IT'S RAINING HONDAS

Everyone loves a rainy day, right? You know, the kind that's windy, blustery, pouring sheets of water that's guaranteed to ruin your shoes and drench the legs of your pants. Sure, everybody loves that, especially on your way *in* to work.

Let's think about rain for a minute. The sun evaporates the water over the oceans. The water vapor rises and forms clouds. The natural winds caused by the rotation of the earth blow the clouds over dry land. When they reach a certain density, there's a cloudburst and it rains. Nothing miraculous about it, right? Just like so many other phenomena of the world, rain looks natural.

Let's see.

About ten years ago, there was a storm in New York City that dropped about 30 inches of snow and freezing rain in about twenty-four hours. For some cities, that's nothing more than a sprinkling, but for New York, that's a national disaster. It took about 2-3 days for us to get almost back to normal. Practically everything was shut down. The kids loved it.

I remember hearing on the radio a few days later that scientists had calculated that approximately twenty million tons of rain and ice fell during that storm. That's the equivalent of dropping ten million Honda Civics onto the streets of New York over a 24-hour period.

Imagine: you get into a helicopter and you get a giant chain with a crane attached to the end of it. You grab a Honda Civic and go up about 3 miles into the sky and then you let it go. It's bound to cause mass destruction. Now do that ten million times! You could wipe out the entire city!

But wait a minute, you may argue, the Honda is concentrated weight, but rain is all spread out. Well, think about that a minute. Whose idea was that? Why doesn't rain fall as one giant sheet of water, like Niagara Falls? Why does it fall in small raindrops that, even in the middle of a summer storm, won't even harm the petal of a rose?

Here's another question. Where were those twenty million tons of water and ice before they fell to the ground? They were floating in mid-air! Does that mean that 19 million tons can float, but twenty million can't?

Who controls this powerful force of nature that has the awesome power to destroy, yet benefits all living creatures? The laws of nature and the laws of physics and everything else that has the power to destroy or the power to build were put here by God, the Creator of the universe.

Where are the great kindnesses in all this? Number one, 99% of the time, this awesome power of rain is used to build, not to destroy, by providing mankind and animals with fresh water. Number two, it provides the proper rains in the proper season to allow plants and food to grow. And number three, how else would the dry cleaners stay in business, if it weren't for all of those rumpled trouser pants after a good rain?

LITTLE GREEN APPLES

Was it Sir Isaac Newton who said, "I wouldn't know what gravity was if it hit me over the head"?

It seems he was in for a surprise. There he was, sitting under the old apple tree, minding his own business, when a ripe, juicy apple plunked down on his head and, well, the rest is history.

It took someone of Isaac Newton's mathematical acumen to tell us exactly how gravity works – mass, distance, particles, acceleration, etc., etc.

But suppose for a moment that it wasn't Isaac Newton, scientist and mathematician, sitting under that apple tree that day, but rather Isaac Newberg, the local philosopher. What might have happened?

He may not have been able to answer the question "how" the apple fell, but he might have asked the question "why" the apple fell. He may have pondered, "That apple has been sitting on that tree for weeks. It's gone through rainstorms and strong winds and it never fell off. And now, after it turned a tantalizing bright red color, it decides to fall on my head. What is this, some kind of wake-up call?"

So he thinks about it. "Did I ever realize before that all fruits – apples, oranges, bananas, plums, peaches, grapes and cherries are all totally green before they ripen, and that they blend in perfectly with the leaves of their trees? Maybe that's so that no one will notice them and pick them until they're ready.

"Did I look at the perfectly packaged, air-tight covering on the apple that seals out bugs and locks in the juices? Maybe that's so it will be fresh and flavorful until I'm ready to eat it.

"Did I appreciate that if I bought too many and didn't finish them all in time, this same packaging turns an ugly brown color to let me know that the apple has overstayed its welcome?

"Have I ever taken advantage of the free coupons inside the apple that entitle me to a lifetime supply of apples? All I have to do is plant them!

"Did I fully understand that within these seeds is the formula to recreate a tree of wood, complete with roots and bark and leaves and blossoms that are capable of producing exact replicas of this tasty fruit, needing no food and nourishment other than water, sunlight and tasteless soil?

"Was I aware that somehow the tree knows how to signal the fruit stem to automatically detach itself from the branch and allow the fruit to gently fall to the ground (or on my head) as soon as the fruit is ripe?

"Come to think of it, there are probably dozens of miracles in each piece of fruit showing the hand of an Intelligent Designer. Sometimes we just need to be bopped on the head to recognize them!"

On the other hand, maybe he wouldn't have pondered at all, but would've just eaten the thing. We'll never know.

Scientists like Sir Isaac Newton can tell us *how* things happen because they choose to focus on the cause and effect of everything. But they don't tell us *why* things happen because they fail to note that behind each cause is the First Cause, God Himself, Who guides this world with plan and purpose.

So you might say that after all is said and done, Newton still really didn't understand *why* there is gravity, even though it did hit him on the head!

A BOY
NAMED JOYCE

What would you do if you were growing up one hundred years ago in New Jersey and your name were Joyce? You probably wouldn't think twice about it. Joyce is a pretty common name: unless you're a boy. Then you might find that there were some guys from the south side of New Brunswick who thought it was pretty funny. And then you would have two options: you could either become a fighter or you could become a poet.

Fortunately for America, Joyce Kilmer decided to become both. He was a daring young fighter in World War 1, killed in action defending his fellow soldiers. Before that, he was a gentle poet.

While serving on the staff of the *New York Times*, he wrote a small collection of poetry. No doubt it would have been far more extensive had he not died at the age of 31.

His best-loved poem is "Trees." It begins:

I think that I shall never see
A poem lovely as a tree.

In this inspiring 12-line tribute, he speaks of the heartwarming sight of the birds in a tree's nest, of the serenity of the snow on a tree's boughs and the graceful majesty of a tree's height.

A great first ten lines. But then he goes and spoils it all by saying something foolish like:

Poems are made by fools like me,
But only God can make a tree.

Why would he say something like that? Everybody knows that a tree just comes from a seed! All you do is put the seed in the ground, wait a couple of weeks, and just before the seed disintegrates completely, up from the ground sprouts a tiny oak, or a birch or a maple tree. So what does that have to do with God? Everybody knows that seeds come from trees. And trees come from seeds. And seeds from trees, from seeds, from trees.

And if you keep saying it enough times, you come to the very first tree, I mean, seed. No, maybe, tree. And all you have to figure out is where that first tree came from. But that should be easy to figure out. (By now you know where I'm going with this.) It probably came from a fish that became an alligator that became a dog that became a tree, and that's how you got a dogwood tree. And all the other types of trees are probably just variations of this same theme.

Or maybe I've got it all wrong. Perhaps there were some idealistic amoebas thousands of years ago that had 20-20 foresight and they knew that there were going to be human beings and that they would want fruit and shade and wood, so they decided that instead of becoming part of the evolutionary tree that leads to people, they would just become part of the tree. And so instead of going the fish-reptile-mammal route, they went the fungus-grass-rose-tree route. Maybe Kilmer should have written "Ode to an Amoeba." (Although, frankly, I doubt it would have sold as well as the one about trees.)

Where did Master Joyce get the idea that there was anything so miraculous about a tree that it could only come from God? Maybe he noticed as a youngster that all of the thousands of leaves on a tree are always arranged with the dark, glossy green side facing up, so they could maximize the effect of the direct rays of the sun in turning life-giving sunlight into food for the tree. And maybe he noticed that for every leaf to perform its function perfectly, one branch never grows directly on top of another.

As a poet, he would have noticed the beauty of the leaves in autumn as they turn their different colors just before they fall. And as he strolled through the meadows over the crunchy leaves under-foot he would have calculated that if he put all of the leaves from a single tree side by side they would cover not one, but several acres of land, yet when they were on the tree they covered an area not bigger than a house. And more astounding is that these miles of leaves would all fit neatly into the flatbed of a pickup truck.

Could he have failed to see that not only doesn't a tree drop its leaves until they are no longer needed for shade or food, but trees also hold onto their blossoms until they're fertilized, to their seeds until they're mature and to their fruits until they're ripe. But they never drop their branches or twigs, because they are the essence of the tree and they are needed for next year.

Could he not but marvel at the prolific powers of a single seed that can organize the materials found in soil and water into a complex, mighty, living organism of roots, leaves, wood, bark and sap that can become a protective home for bees, woodpeckers and squirrels?

Maybe when Joyce looked at a tree he truly understood that what he saw could not have evolved by a simple, undirected flow of nature. It was far too beautiful, far too wondrous, and far too harmonious with the rest of the world to have developed by acci-dent. That is when he came to the realization from deep within him, that only God could make a tree.

Now, would he have thought of all that, if his name had been Irving

LIFE IN
THE 'BURBS

've always been a city boy. I was born in Brooklyn and work in Manhattan. So when I got married, I decided to move to the suburbs. Instead of looking for a house in Borough Park or Williamsburg, I moved to Flatbush, where practically every home has a private driveway and a green lawn in the front. (For a city boy, that's considered the suburbs.)

And thus began my career as a farmer. In my one-sixteenth-of-an-acre farm (actually a little less, because the house takes up most of the lot), I raise tomatoes, cucumbers and occasionally green peppers. In a good year, I can actually get six or seven tomatoes out of a season. It's such a rewarding experience.

And then there's my front lawn. Stretching a luxurious four feet by eight feet, I grow what I consider to be grass. My neighbors tell me it's a specific breed called crab grass, but then they know a lot more of that technical stuff than I do.

But my real love is my flower garden. I plant the annuals – impatiens and geraniums and black-eyed suzies. Creating the vista of color and depth are the perennials – daylilies and zinnias and rhododendrons. They're my pride and joy.

I marvel at how every year the perennials know exactly when spring starts and they begin growing and flowering all on their own. The bigger wonder to me is, how do they manage to live through the winter? Some of those days are freezing! At least I can wear my wool socks, wool suit and wool gloves.

Wool, of course, naturally keeps you warm; but not by generating its own heat (the body does that). Wool is fluffy and airy so it serves as an insulator to prevent the heat of the body from escaping.

So what do plants do?

There's something else that does the same thing as wool. It's called snow. It comes down in flakes, each one individually designed with six points. They interlock one with the other, but not perfectly. Just like someone playing Tetris for the first time, there are always spaces between the pieces. Much of the snow on the ground after a storm consists of empty space. That space prevents the heat of the soil from escaping just like wool prevents body heat from escaping. By doing that, not only does it protect my flowers from freezing, it also protects all the ants, earthworms, fungi and bacteria that enrich and enliven the soil. (Let's assume we want to protect those things. They have a right to live too, ya know.)

It not only protects plants and animals, snow also prevents the underground water lines from freezing. And it gives us some great winter sports to enjoy and it provides us with incomparable scenery in the mountains and fjords around the world.

And you know, somehow, that sparkling white color adds to the beauty. The color makes sense, too. Red snow would be too glaring on the eyes, blue would just blend in with the sky, black would attract too much heat and would melt too quickly, and we all know about yellow snow.

Another thing: guys like me aren't the only ones excited about snow. Farmers rejoice too, because without snow, there would be no winter wheat. Snow prevents the soil from freezing solid so that water is able to penetrate all winter long, and an entire crop can be saved. Finally, as the snow gradually melts it seeps into the ground, soaking the soil instead of running off the way rain does. First it acts like a blanket and then a nutrient – sort of like having your cake and then eating it too.

And while it seems to us city boys that it takes just too darn long for the snow to melt, we will just have to continue sloshing through this magnificent, purposeful gift from our Creator, year after year.

So the next time you're upset about digging the car out of the snow, just think about my flowers and remember: spring is just around the corner.

THE WAKE-UP CALL

Nobody likes a wake-up call – and I'm not even talking philosophically. Ask any businessman who travels for a living. There is nothing more annoying at 6:00 o'clock in the morning than a cheery-voiced desk clerk telling you it's time to get up.

There's another type of wake-up call. If you have a six-year-old at home, you know what I mean. No sooner does a thunderstorm begin than he's at the foot of your bed, shaking your foot and telling you that he's scared. And no matter how many times you tell him that it's only God snoring, or the upstairs neighbors bowling, he still won't go back to bed until it's over.

As we all know, the booming sound of thunder is only noise. So what is this wake-up call of thunder announcing?

Simply, the greatness of one of God's creations – lightning. And what is so great about lightning, besides the fact that it makes the perfect background for a murder-mystery? Consider this.

There's a verse in Psalms 135 stating that, "God made the lightning for the rain." A great twentieth-century thinker, Rabbi Avigdor Miller, explains that this refers to the fact that rain needs lightning in order to accomplish one of its jobs. What did he mean by that?

I know from my farm in Brooklyn that if I want my tomatoes to grow, I have to water them (which is one of the purposes of rain). But if I want them to be really big and juicy, I have to use Miracle-Gro, or at least some type of fertilizer. Water only helps the chemical reactions take place, but a plant still needs healthy soil to grow in. And since soil is only a few inches deep anywhere in the world, its nutrients get used up fairly quickly and need to be replenished. That's where fertilizers come in. And they come in a variety of different types, potencies and smells.

What do they all have in common, though? Nitrates, which is a combination of oxygen and nitrogen. There's only one problem, and that is that nitrogen is practically inert: it doesn't combine easily with other chemicals. The only way to overcome this problem is to use intense heat to fuse it together with oxygen. Since the farmers of the world haven't the time to go running around with Bunsen burners looking for spare nitrogen, God does the job for them. Each time that lightning strikes, the intense heat generated by this electrical reaction causes the nitrogen in the air to combine with oxygen. These gases, combined with the traces of ammonia in the air, dissolve into the rain, which then brings this life-giving fertilizer into the soil.

Score a point for the Psalmist.

But don't think that you have to wait for a thunderstorm for lightning to happen. Lightning is taking place continually in the atmosphere every day in order to keep our soil rich and healthy.

Thunder is God's reminder to us that even when we are too busy to take care of the things we need to survive, the benevolent Creator of the world is ably taking care of them Himself. So the next time you hear a clap of thunder, wake up and smell the fertilizer.

UNDER CONSTRUCTION

At the northern end of Manhattan is the neighborhood known as Harlem. For almost 100 years it has been home to the Apollo Theatre, Aretha Franklin, rap music, drugs, crime and now Bill Clinton. In an attempt to revitalize the area, developers have started building huge luxury condominium complexes. One in particular is "to die for" – duplex accommodations with sprawling living rooms, wood-burning fireplaces, picture windows overlooking the Hudson River, private patios, sense-surround stereo, self-vacuuming floors, ultra-modern kitchens, computerized climate control, private bathrooms in every bedroom, twelve-foot high ceilings and a spiral staircase to the second floor. Everything is standard equipment and could be customized to suit your individual taste, all for one low price.

Almost makes you want to move to Harlem! (Well, let's not get carried away.)

Did you ever think about what goes into building a structure like that? First of all, you have all of the brainpower of the architects, builders and craftsmen. They have to plan, design and execute everything perfectly, right down to the last detail: things like the doors, the doorknobs, the door locks, the lighting fixtures, the kitchen cabinets, the floor tiles, the bathroom tiles, the toilet paper holder, wall colors, floor colors, rug colors, apartment layout, fixture design, lobby design, the elevators, the up and down buttons for the elevators, the computer that runs the elevators, the computer that runs the climate control, the soundproofing, the waterproofing, the burglar proofing, the picture windows, the patio doors, the patio railings, the electrical wiring, the air conditioning vents, the cooling system, the heating system, the spiral staircase, the hole in the ceiling for the spiral staircase and the little peep hole in the front door so you know who's coming to visit. No small job.

And second of all, think of all of the different materials that are needed for this: concrete, cement, bricks, plaster, wood, steel, copper, aluminum, iron, brass, glass, fiberglass, marble, formica, vinyl, glue, paint, plastic, rubber, cotton and wool.

We've certainly come a long way since mankind lived in huts and tents made out of animal hide. I wonder, why didn't they build luxury apartments back then? It could be for one of four reasons:

They didn't have the need.

They didn't have the know-how.

They didn't have the materials.

They actually liked living in huts.

Let's see.

It's an historical fact that cities and communal living began about 5,500 years ago. Back at that time, the population consisted of Adam, Eve, a few animals and some snake in the grass. As the population rapidly grew, there was enough space for tents and primitive homes to be built on unlimited tracts of land. There was no reason to build up when you could build out. (There is one story, however, about some people who babbled about building the world's first skyscraper, but I understand they didn't wind up living there for long.)

Even traffic jams during city rush hours were limited to a few oxen caught off the side of a muddy road. In addition, most of humanity lived in temperate climates, so they didn't have to blow the budget on heating bills to protect themselves from the elements.

As the need arose, mankind utilized its know-how. Unlike animals, mankind was able to use ever-expanding, superior intellect to develop tools, artifacts and building materials. That's where we got the names Stone Age, Bronze Age and Iron Age. Animals usually never develop beyond Old Age.

Housing soon became more sophisticated and intricate. Mud and stone houses replaced tents, only to be further refined into multi-story homes of bricks and clay. Animals also became domesticated and began living in shelters – either homes or barns – but they relied on man to build them. Their building skills continue to be limited to dams, hives, cocoons and nests.

As cities grew, so did man's innovations. From houses of bricks and clay, mankind eventually learned to include the use of wood, then iron, then heating, then electricity, then plumbing and then air conditioning. Then repairmen.

There's no telling where the future will lead us. But one thing is obvious: the materials we use have always been here. The world was created with all of the ingredients necessary to build everything from a primitive hut to the most complex skyscraper. Even synthetic materials such as rubber, plastic and glass ultimately are made from naturally occurring resources.

And not only the materials for shelter are provided, we also have everything we need for clothing, transportation, computing, communicating and entertainment.

Animals don't use them. Animals don't need them, only mankind does. And as time goes by, we will no doubt learn how to use all of the materials found here on Earth for the benefit of mankind. Where would we be without this unparalleled kindness from our Creator?

Probably not in Harlem.

IT'S A GAS

'm not that big on technology.

I was one of the last people in Brooklyn to get rid of my rotary-dial phone. (Some of my kids' friends had actually never seen one until they came to our house.) Cell phones, portable email and the Internet just don't *do* anything for me. But there is one bit of technology that does get me excited.

Refrigerators.

Let's look inside one. (Don't try this at home. Trust me.) They have a compressor in the back of them – that motor that goes on every time you open the door. It compresses a gas called freon and stores it in the refrigerator coils. Then, when the temperature in the fridge gets too high, the freon starts to expand inside the coils. Like all gases, when it expands, it cools. But freon doesn't just get cool, it can freeze!

Did you ever have to empty all the food in the freezer 'cause your wife couldn't find the hamburger buns that she just *knew* were in there? That stuff is cold!

Thank you, Mr. Westinghouse, or maybe Mr. Frigidaire, for coming up with an idea like this. But how did freon learn how to do this? Where does freon come from?

Glad you asked. Freon happens to be one of the 92 naturally occurring elements in the universe. It's number 87 on the Periodic Table of Elements and is a gas just like hydrogen, oxygen and carbon dioxide, except that it's inert (even more inert than nitrogen) – which means it can't do anything. At least that's what we thought for many years.

Freon is also considerably more rare than those other gases but, then again, we don't have as many refrigerators on Earth as we do human beings, so we don't need as much. But who would have thought back when the world began that one hot day in August all you would want to do is sit in your air-conditioned den and sip an ice-cold soda – and that you would need freon to do that?

I couldn't have thought of that. Could you have thought of that? To think ahead like that, you'd have to be omniscient or something.

Exactly. In His infinite wisdom, the Creator of the universe provided mankind with everything that we would ever need to achieve maximum pleasure in this world – from the air we breathe, to the water we drink, to the freon that cools them both. It must be great to be all-knowing.

Me, I would settle for just knowing if it's going to rain tomorrow, and maybe a good course in technology.

THE 11ᵀᴴ COMMANDMENT

I once read that every day Americans consume enough soda to fill up a bottle the size of the Empire State Building. (Have you noticed that it even looks like an old bottle of Pepsi?) And since all that soda comes in bottles, cans and cups, that's an awful lot of garbage to dispose of.

Hence, the 11ᵗʰ Commandment: Thou Shalt Recycle.

Driving to work on Tuesday mornings, besides dodging a battalion of school buses picking up kids on every street corner, I also have to wait behind the big, bulky garbage trucks as sanitation men sift through the multiple sets of garbage cans in front of every house to pick up the recycling – one can for newspapers, magazines, cardboard boxes, third-class mail and cereal boxes; another one for cans, bottles, jugs, jars and used aluminum foil.

Two things about recycling:

Everybody agrees that it's absolutely necessary.

Everybody agrees that it's absolutely a pain in the neck.

I haven't yet met anyone who gets a surge of patriotic fever when he separates normal garbage from recyclables – although I'll bet he's out there somewhere.

I'm sure the Democrats would love to take credit for this great Earth-saving concept, but some say it started happening in outer space quite a few years before the Dems ever came on the scene. As the theory goes, hydrogen and helium atoms fuse to form stars (like our Sun), which then make something useful out of them like carbon, oxygen, freon, iron, lead and gold. When the stars finish doing all the upgrading they can, they explode – sending out stardust and gases millions of miles into space only to begin the process all over again. It's what you might call the longest recycling job in history!

Hey, I'll drink to that. Maybe I'll even drink something exotic, like Original Ancient Water. (It's a lot healthier for you than fourteen-year-old Scotch, unless you live in New Jersey.)

Of course, water appeared early in the Earth's history. And the water we have now is the same water we had thousands of years ago. We've added a few pollutants like oil spills, sunken ships and radioactive waste, but thanks to the eternal rain cycle, by and large our water today is just as pure as it was at the beginning. How's that for recycling!

We water plants so we can eat them. Did you know that the Earth's soil is only a few inches deep all around the world, and that in some places, all the soil has been washed or blown away and all you have left is sand?

How come we haven't used up all of the soil on the Earth? You got it – recycling does it again. Plants that rot, leaves that fall, humans and animals that die all return to the soil to replenish and fertilize it. It's a constant cycle to ensure that plants and food never run out.

Without plants, we couldn't exist (although it would end suppertime squabbles over spinach). Animals wouldn't have food and grass to eat. We would not only be out of spinach, but we'd lose all our steaks, chicken cutlets and eggs too.

We also wouldn't have air to breathe! That's because we breathe in oxygen and exhale carbon dioxide. Plants breathe in carbon dioxide and give off oxygen. A mere coincidence? Think about it.

How long do you think you could go without air? Two minutes, three minutes? Probably. Twenty minutes? Well, you might, but I don't think you'd enjoy the experience. Every animal, every plant, every human being needs air to survive. With over 5 billion people in the world and billions of four-legged animals in the world, an awful lot of air is needed.

Yet it doesn't seem like anybody is lacking for air. Ever been to Europe? They have air there. Same thing in South America. Los Angeles? Ok, maybe not in LA. But you get the gist: Wherever you go in the world, you're going to find air. The entire Earth, from pole to pole and everywhere in between, has naturally occurring, chemically suitable, fresh air. Sounds to me like another phenomenal job of recycling!

Ask a few people, "What is the most precious commodity in the world?" A Hollywood starlet might tell you jewelry – you know, gold and diamonds – or maybe husbands. A scientist might tell you radioactive isotopes, to produce the nuclear fuel we need to power the world. A child might say television or ice cream.

I'll put my money on air – the most precious commodity and yet the most abundant.

The Earth has limited resources, yet through these many years, those things that we need most are in constant supply. We have some through the ingenuity of man, like soda cans and copier paper, but the really big things were taken care of long ago, before we ever got here. The recycling systems were put into place by a Master Planner Who knew what we would need and Who knew how to balance things perfectly.

What wisdom and kindness it takes to see to it that the Earth isn't overrun with water in the same way it is covered with air, and that air is not concentrated in a few places like water. He has set up the world in such a way that our most basic requirements are available in the exact ratio that they're needed.

In fact, He sustains our lives through a series of cycles and recycles:

Gases, stars, supernovae, gases.

Oceans, clouds, rain, oceans.

Seeds, plants, fruits, seeds.

Oxygen, carbon dioxide, oxygen.

Food, energy, fertilizer, food.

Sleep, refresh, awake, sleep.

Summer, fall, winter, spring.

Birth, life, death, rebirth.

There is an eternal cycle on both the physical and the non-physical level that transcends us all. So when we recycle, we are really just following His example.

Did you ever think that separating garbage could be so noble?

How Big a Bang?

WHY IS
THE SKY BLUE?

t's easy for theologians and those who grew up in religious homes to understand and accept the Biblical account of Creation. There is a benevolent God Who chose to create a universe. He created everything in six days, and He continues to watch over His creations like a loving Father to His children.

It's not as easy for someone like a scientist, who is skeptical about accepting things without proof. Faith alone doesn't work in this modern version of the Age of Reason.

However, there is a group of respected scientists who are entertaining the possibility that, not only does this world have an intelligent Designer, but also that this universe was brought into existence specifically for the purpose of bringing about an intelligent mankind. This theory, known as the " Anthropic Principle," concludes that this universe is so finely tuned and the coincidences are so numerous that the nature of its existence cannot be a chance event.

They base their theory on the fact that if even one of the constants of nature, such as the speed of light or the force of gravity, were changed by the most minute amount, it is unlikely that stars or planets or any type of life that we could imagine would ever have come into existence.

Dr. Paul Davies, who is a Professor of Theoretical Studies at Newcastle University in England, said:

"The really amazing thing is not that life on earth is balanced on a knife edge, but that the entire universe is balanced on a knife edge and would be total chaos if any of the constants of nature were off even slightly. You see, even if you dismiss man as a chance happening, the fact remains the universe seems unreasonably suited to the existence of life, almost contrived."

Many people would think at this point, "Maybe this universe just happened to come about, and if we were a different kind of being we could also say, 'We're here, so that proves God must have created the universe.' In fact, maybe it didn't have to be this universe; it could have been something else. Maybe we're using 20-20 hindsight when we say, 'Since we're here, there must be a God.'"

Most of us have actually asked a question like that when we were growing up and got the same circular answer.

"Daddy, why is the sky blue?"

"Because if it were green you would ask me why the sky is green."

But Dr. David Deutsch from Oxford University answers the question from his scientific perspective, making it clear that it couldn't be any different.

"If we nudge one of the constants just a few percent in one direction, stars burn out within millions of years of their formation and there is no time for evolution. If we nudge them a few percent in the other direction, then no elements heavier than helium form. No carbon, no life, not even any chemistry, no complexity at all."

In other words, these scientists believe that we had to have this universe. It had to develop exactly this way, otherwise there wouldn't be planets, there wouldn't be life.

One could argue that maybe it was still just by chance. This doesn't necessarily mean that there was any outside force directing this.

Sir Fred Hoyle, the eminent British astronomer, is part of this group, puzzling over the issue of our beginnings. He agrees that the universe is finely-tuned, but he also stated that in the early formation of the universe,

"...there were *numerous, one-time, fortunate* occurrences that seem to indicate that *purposeful* adjustments had been made in the laws of physics and chemistry in order to produce the elements needed to support life."

Look at some of the phrases he used to try to understand the origin of the cosmos and the ultimate appearance of mankind.

He speaks of occurrences that are:

...*numerous*, meaning more than one (probably a lot more than one);

...*one-time*, i.e. they only happened once. Scientists never speak of one-time phenomena because that goes against the principle of science that says that the way things occur in nature today is the way they have always occurred.

...*fortunate*...Of all of the billions of possibilities that could have happened to the detriment of the universe, those which occurred "one time" each were beneficial. (You might want to consider the use of the word "miracles" here.)

...*purposeful* ... Whose purpose could it have been to "produce the elements needed to support life"? The gases'? The stars'? Why should they care?

Here is where the scientists get off, as their discipline does not speculate on questions like "who?" Theologians, however, answer that there is a benevolent Creator, an intelligent Designer Who chose to create a universe with the ultimate purpose of creating mankind, upon whom He could bestow His goodness and who would serve Him by presiding over an ethical, harmonious world.

According to Hoyle, they must be right.

TWINKLE, TWINKLE, LITTLE STAR

Twinkle, twinkle, little star,
How I wonder what you are.

In case you're *still* wondering what they are, you're probably old enough now to hear the truth. Stars are giant balls of gas that release tons of energy each second as they fuse hydrogen and helium atoms to form the heavier elements of the universe.

Takes away some of the mystery and romance, doesn't it?

By the way, which star do you think the poet was looking at? Scientists tell us that there are 100,000 million stars in our galaxy, the Milky Way, and 100,000 million galaxies in the universe. So that's a lot of choices.

As far as I'm concerned, there's only one star worth singing about and that's the sun. It rises majestically in the east every morning and gives off its brilliant display of colors in the west each evening.

Why do I think that the sun is so special? I have a few reasons:

Number One – It's Awesome

It provides mankind with over 120 trillion horsepower of energy each second in the form of life-giving light.

Number Two – It's Miraculous

Sunlight causes soil, air and rain to combine in such a way that they transform from inorganic states to become organic vegetation for man and animals to feed on. Do you know how it does that? Nobody does.

Number Three – It's Enlightening

It literally lights up our lives by revealing to us the beauty of the world and the universe by triggering the sensations of color, size and form in our brains.

Number Four – It's Humble

It's not the only show in town. If it shined continuously for twenty-four hours a day, our bodies, our fields and our oceans would wither away under the incessant beating down of the sun's strong rays. So it gives us a break and shares the spotlight with the moon.

Number Five – It's Mysterious

Its light defies all laws of science and nature by mysteriously acting as matter *or* energy *or* both at the same time, depending literally on how you look at it.

Number Six – It's More Mysterious

Light travels at the same speed relative to you whether or not *you* are moving and whether or not the source of light is moving. That means that even if you're in a spacecraft traveling directly towards the sun at thousands of miles per hour, the light of the sun approaches you at the same 186,000 miles per second as if you were standing still. Do you know why? Nobody does.

Number Seven – It's Considerate

It provides us with the means to measure days, months and years. Imagine if life were just one long day and your in-laws decided to come over for the weekend – there'd be no getting rid of them.

Number Eight – It's Fleeting

The sun is not going to last forever. Scientists estimate that at the current rate of converting 5,000 tons of mass into energy every second, the sun will only last another 5.4 billion years. So if you're planning a vacation to a warm climate, you'd better go soon.

Number Nine – It's Fortuitous

None of these miracles would be possible if we were just a few thousand miles closer or further from the sun – we would either be "toast"y warm or "frost"y cold.

And how many thousands is "a few thousand"? Talking mathematics for a moment, the radius of the Earth is about 4,000 miles. So that means that if the North Pole were truly north (whatever direction that means), the Equator would be 4,000 miles closer to the sun than the North Pole. The average temperature at the North Pole is 7 degrees Fahrenheit and at the Equator it's 102 degrees, a difference of 95 degrees. So, all other things being equal, if we were just 4,000 miles closer to the sun, even San Diego would be a tepid 167 degrees in the shade and the Atlantic and Pacific Oceans would be nothing more than ancient memories. If the sun is 93 million miles away, that's a fine tuning of 0.00043. Lucky break, no?

And finally, Number Ten – It Makes You Wonder

Ultimately, the sun hints to us of the awesome power of a Creator Who can use just one out of the ten billion trillion fiery lights of the sky to be His humble servant to an inquisitive mankind.

Maybe it's no coincidence that "Twinkle, Twinkle" is the first nursery rhyme we ever learn as tots. It's a pretty "star"tling subject.

THE THEORY OF EVERYTHING

Scientists have long been searching for the one formula that would explain how everything in the universe works. It would be called the Theory of Everything. However, every time they arrive at one conclusion, something always pops up that renders their original conclusion invalid. So the formula is adjusted again and then something else is inconsistent. Physicists, astronomers and chemists all over the world have devoted thousands of hours and billions of research dollars to come up with an all-encompassing, universal explanation of everything, all to no avail.

Professor John Archibald Wheeler of Princeton University expressed their collective frustration when he said:

"There must be at the bottom of it all, not a simple equation, but an utterly simple idea. And to me, that idea, when we finally discover it, will be so compelling and so inevitable and beautiful, we will all say, 'How could it have ever been otherwise?'"

Let's see if we can help him out.

Since most of us don't have nuclear microscopes in our basements and probably will never look through the Hubble telescope to analyze new star formations, let's see if we can use a little rational thinking about what this "simple idea" might be.

A baby forming in its mother's womb must develop from a single fertilized egg into a complex being having trillions of cells at the time of birth. A full-grown adult has about 30 trillion cells, but this growth in size is nothing compared to the intricate task of developing bones, organs, skin, intelligence and emotions from a single cell.

Together, these cells must form a total of ten trillion connections with the brain, and in almost every baby ever born this is done correctly. All of this is accomplished through the functioning of DNA, the computer program that runs every living organism on earth – plants, animals and mankind.

Did you ever consider what DNA is made of? In biology parlance they're called nucleic acids, and they are a specialized form of amino acids, which are basically proteins. Proteins are made up of carbon, hydrogen, and oxygen. Carbon, hydrogen and oxygen are made up of atoms. Atoms are made up of protons, neutrons and electrons.

But stop and think for a moment, how does an atom know where to go to make ten trillion connections? (I have trouble even finding my way through a New York City train station.)

Since when did we ever attribute intelligence to an atom? Where is this intelligence coming from that gives DNA the foresight to tell an electron where to go? If every atom acted independently, there would be an infinite array of biological species. Since this is clearly not the case, we are forced to conclude that there is a Unified Intelligence acting upon the most minute particles of the universe, coordinating every action and reaction.

There is a phrase that has been included in the Jewish daily prayers that are said in the morning. It refers to God as the All-Powerful force that renews continually the workings of the creation of the world every day, through His everlasting goodness. In other words, the prayer says that we are sustained through the intelligence, the design and the desire of the Creator of the world.

The more one delves into the hidden, deep workings of the universe the more he will find that there is only One answer to how Everything works.

An "utterly simple idea," no?

DOUBLE TALK?

Don't take my word for it on this because it is too hard to believe. Check it out for yourself.

There is a standard scientific experiment that has been duplicated in hundreds of laboratories around the world. It leaves scientists puzzled, as indeed it should. It's called simply "The Double Slit Experiment."

To conduct the experiment you need a few basic items. The first is sunlight, the second is a type of flashlight called a maser gun. Then you need a piece of cardboard with two thin slits in it (hence the name of the experiment), and finally a piece of photographic film to record how the light is coming through the slits.

The experiment is performed in several different ways. The first time, one of the slits is closed and sunlight is allowed to shine through the other slit. When the light passes through, it hits the film behind it and, as you would expect, there is an exposed line directly behind the slit, but it has fuzzy edges. The fuzziness is because of the slight diffraction (bending) of the wave of light as it passed through the opening. When you repeat the experiment with the other slit open and the first one closed, you get the same results.

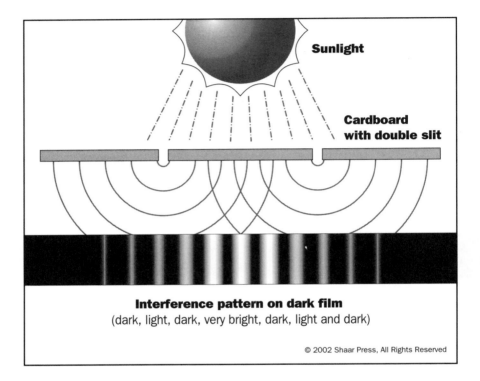

Interference pattern on dark film
(dark, light, dark, very bright, dark, light and dark)

In the second experiment, both slits are open. Here, instead of getting two fuzzy lines, you wind up with a series of dark, light, dark, very bright, dark, light and dark areas. Scientists explain that this is due to the fact that light is a wave, and as the waves pass through the slits they are diffracted: as the two sets of waves expand beyond the slits, they either cancel each other out (dark spots), reinforce each other (very bright) or result in a combination somewhere in between. This experiment proves beyond a "shadow" of a doubt that light is a wave.

The only problem is that Albert Einstein proved that light is a particle, which means it's a distinct entity of matter. Let's see how that works.

For this part of the experiment, we take that maser gun flashlight and adjust it so that only one particle of light is emitted at a time (perfectly doable in a physics lab, as Einstein and others have shown). Perform the experiment with only one slit open and you get the same fuzzy line. Open the other and close the first, same fuzzy line. Open both and you get the same wave pattern again.

Hold it! How can you get the wave pattern? We just said that light is a particle! Not only that, there is nothing to cancel because matter doesn't cancel matter, only waves do! Furthermore, we're only releasing one particle at a time, so even if it were a wave, how could such a thing happen?

So you say to yourself, maybe something funny is going on here. So you put a monitor on one of the slits to determine if it's really a particle going through it or if it's a wave. Indeed, the monitor detects that one full particle is going through the slit. But now, since you put the monitor on, instead of getting the wave pattern again as you just did (dark, light, dark, very bright, dark, light and dark), you're getting the two fuzzy line patterns as if first one of the slits were opened and the other closed, and then vice versa, as in our first experiment.

It seems as if the light not only knows that it is being watched, but it can feel when there is one slit open or two. Light, energy, photons, electrons, no matter what you call them, can't know anything. And furthermore, why should they care if we're watching?

Wait a minute. They can't care because, even if we say they're intelligent, we never said they're emotional. (Maybe that's what they mean by "mood" lighting.)

Yet they definitely seem to know and care. You can understand why scientists are puzzled. This wave/particle duality of light has both scientific and philosophical implications. If we look at light as a wave, it's a wave. If we assume it's a particle and if we measure it as such, it's a particle. We see the world as we assume it exists.

Philosophically, when we are tied to our physical bodies, we view this world as a physical entity. If we were to leave our bodies and enter the spiritual world, we would then be capable of viewing this world as spirit, or energy. Thousands have experienced this "near death" experience and testified to a world of love, warmth and light where time ceases to exist.

But a person doesn't have to "almost" die in order to touch spiritual dimensions. We can all get glimpses of it when we look at the beauty of a sunset, or the massive expanse of the heavenly stars, or the awesome power of a hurricane or the perfection and miracle of a newborn baby.

These are all aspects of the Infinite Source of all energy in the world. They can be perceived as physical phenomenon, or we can measure them as energy and become energized.

Wave or particle, nature or miracles – it's all in how you choose to see them.

E=mc?

Remember Rumpelstiltskin? Depending on which version of the tale you saw, he was an elf, an imp, a grinch or some other kind of monster. His claim to fame was that he helped a (future) princess spin straw into gold, in exchange for her firstborn. Nasty business tactics, but you've got to admit that converting straw into gold is a pretty neat talent.

No one has ever figured out how to actually do that, though alchemists tried for years. Even Einstein didn't figure it out, though he had a head start, knowing how something can convert from one thing into something totally different. His formula, $E=mc^2$, revolutionized the way that both matter and energy are viewed. He was even named Man of the Century for his discovery.

Not to take anything away from Albert, but we've been doing this kind of thing for years. Ask any athlete who ever drank a glass of orange juice before a track meet, or a mother who let her kids have too many cookies before bedtime, or someone who just enjoyed his meal after fasting all day. They took the matter from the food that they ate and converted it into jolts of energy. And we don't stop there. We even take this energy and convert it back into matter by exercising (muscle cells) or by watching television (fat cells). It's not exactly what Einstein was referring to but, nonetheless, the duality of all matter and energy as two sides of the same coin has been utilized by living beings since the beginning of time.

But consider his formula for a moment. It states that any object, no matter how big or small, can generate enormous amounts of energy if its atoms are blasted apart. This discovery, in essence, helped create the atom bomb. When we think about "the bomb," we think of fighter planes and cyclotrons and radioactive uranium. But Einstein is referring to something much more basic than that. He states clearly that every atom in existence has potential energy locked inside of it. Yet we see from things all around us that atoms remain in perfect balance as particles of matter for centuries on end and never break down into energy.

We, too, are made up of atoms. We have megatons of energy, *real* energy, trapped within our bodies. In fact, every pencil, every building, every flower, animal and grain of sand has this energy within it. All of the tens of billions of stars of the universe have this energy. Only an infinitesimal amount of energy is used to light up the night sky for us, and the balance remains as potential energy.

How much energy are we talking about? Assuming the average person weighs 150 pounds (without last night's potato chips) and there are over five billion people in the world, then we all contain on the order of ten trillion, trillion, trillion volts of energy locked up inside of us. And that's only counting people. What about the actual mass of the Earth, the sun, and all of the stars and galaxies of the universe? The number is too staggering to calculate.

Where did all of this energy come from? Could it all have originated from a minute speck of matter and energy? How does it remain stable? What prevents the matter of all physical objects from converting instantaneously into energy?

Logic dictates that there must be a source of all energy, a supplier, a generator and a controller. But Einstein tells us that neither matter nor energy can ever be destroyed or created by natural means. So how do we account for the origin of such a massive amount of energy that exists today?

Again logic dictates that the "supplier" must be an infinite source of energy that produced the original energy and sustains the existence of the universe. What form this energy takes would be determined by the will of this Source. Everything we see and use – the Earth, sun, moon, stars, plants, food, animals, gravity, electromagnetism, nuclear power, to name just a few – are all different forms of energy. Converting one type of energy into another is not something that we do on our own; it is the job of an Almighty.

God must be pretty smart.

OPTICAL ILLUSIONS

Have you ever been driving down the highway behind a guy who wasn't driving fast enough above the speed limit, so you decide to pass him? You check your side view mirror, signal to change lanes and start edging over. No sooner do you begin crossing over the white line than the guy next to you gives you the horn and you immediately swerve back into your lane.

Where did he come from? Why didn't you see him?

As every driver knows, you have a blind spot just behind the left passenger door, and if you don't turn around and look before you change lanes, you could be in trouble.

The human eye also has a blind spot. That's because the place where the optic nerve attaches itself to the back of the eyeball doesn't have any rods and cones to register light sensations. Octopuses don't have this problem because their optic nerves are fully integrated with their eyes, but then again, they also have to keep track of eight arms. But most mammals have blind spots.

Did you ever see the old card trick where somebody gives you the ace of spades and tells you to hold it in front of one eye and slowly move it towards and then away from you? When the card gets to a certain spot, the black spade in the center of the card disappears. That's because of your blind spot. Some people call that magic; some people call it an optical illusion. Others just call it science. The reality is that the spade was always there, you just couldn't see it.

I'd like you to try an experiment. (You don't have to do it now, though.) Take a piece of paper about the size of a playing card. Draw thick grid lines horizontally and vertically across the card, spaced about ½″ apart. Near the center of the card, where any two lines intersect, draw a circle about the size of the ace of spades. Now do the same thing, tromboning in and out with the card. You will find that, once again, the circle or spade will disappear. But notice that the grid lines beneath the circle remained! How come? What about your blind spot?

It seems that even though your eye "lifted" the spot off the card, your brain filled in the blanks. It determined that the lines actually belonged there, so it did you a favor and kept them there. Is that the reality? Clearly not. The card (if you drew it properly) consisted of grid lines and a spot. Why should one disappear and the other remain?

People like illusionists David Copperfield and Harry Houdini have been telling us for years that the hand is quicker than the eye. And even though people from Missouri will tell you that seeing is believing, what you see is not always what's really there, or not there.

Coincidentally, scientists are now telling us the same thing. What we see, or think we see, is not always reality.

Allow me to explain. Scientists have recently discovered that all atoms in the universe are 97% empty space. This means that the chair you're sitting on and the book in your hands, and even your hands themselves, are 97% not there. They say that if the Empire State Building were reduced to the actual volume of its physical matter (by removing the space in each atom), it would fit into a space the size of a coffee cup. So why do we sense physical matter? How do we perceive a universe? What is reality?

Suppose for a moment you were blindfolded and escorted into an empty room. When the blindfolds were removed, you sensed that you were wearing a pair of glasses. When you looked around you, everything appeared to be pink. How would you know if the walls themselves were pink or only appeared to be pink because you might be wearing a set of pink glasses? If you couldn't remove the glasses for whatever reason and you couldn't cheat by looking out of the sides of the lenses, you would never know the real color of the walls.

This might seem like an unusual experience, yet in a somewhat similar manner, an element of uncertainty enters into all of our knowledge of the world. In order for us to know something, we first have to perceive it and then pass along the sensations to our brains for understanding. But this understanding is based on the structure of the human mind and therefore we can't necessarily assume that what we perceive is a true reflection of the real nature of the world. (Are the walls pink or do we see them as pink?)

Looking at more walls won't help because we would be using the same standard of comparison that may not have any basis in fact in the first place. The problem is that our minds have a natural tendency to assume that all of the phenomenon of the world can be explained rationally. The laws and principles of science are based on the way scientists perceive the likely effect of a set of causes. But because these results are being analyzed by a human mind, we can still never be sure why a ball falls to the ground or if, in fact, it will continue to do so 100% of the time.

Rabbi Samson Raphael Hirsch, one of the most brilliant writers and educators of the 19th century, wrote,

"Without the belief in the spiritual aspect of the universe, scientists could never be sure that they are not deducing dream from dream and proving dream by dream."

According to this, the reason we perceive a universe is because everywhere we look, in everything we sense, God fills in the blanks. He allows us to feel, hear, see and smell only those things that He wants us to experience.

The conception of an orderly and meaningful existence, therefore, can only be based on the view that there is an all-powerful, all-knowing Creator and Ruler of the universe Who sees true reality. Scientists only *assume* that there is a rational world for us to experience, but they can't prove it because, hey, they're only human.

Put in simpler terms, if you're having a bad day, don't blame the boss; it's God Who's in charge. If, on the other hand, you're having a good day, it's because God has given you a pair of rose-colored glasses for a while. You're being allowed to perceive those pleasurable moments in a physical existence, or so it appears.

One of
a Kind

BABY TEETH

R emember what it's like handling a newborn baby? You know, those cute, adorable little bundles of screaming selfishness? We love them and pamper them (depending on which brand we use) for weeks on end and then after about six months, suddenly they're people! They laugh, they giggle, they recognize you, respond to you, they become almost human!

That lasts for about 2 months. And then it starts all over again. Drooling, ear aches, drippy noses, screaming through the night, grabbing things and putting them in their mouths. You think she has a cold, a virus. But everyone knows – she's teething.

Night after night for weeks and weeks, just when you think she's going to fall asleep, she starts screaming again in agony. By the way, doctors say that teething is a very painful experience. (I don't know how they know this; they probably just asked a kid.)

Then one morning, when you're feeding her that delicious rice cereal mixed with Similac, you hear the spoon go "chink." You look in her mouth and, sure enough, there's her first little tooth just poking its head through the bottom gums. You call your husband at work – "Danny, Danny, the baby just got her first tooth!" You call your mother, your mother-in-law, your best friends. Everyone is so excited about baby's first tooth.

Several weeks later, along comes the next tooth – a month or two later, the next one, and then the fourth one. Four front teeth, two on the top and two on the bottom. And then it stops for the next few months. When it starts again, it's usually with a lot more pain, but always with a lot less fanfare.

You know how at the bowling alleys they have these automatic pin-setting machines? After you throw the second ball, the slide comes down, sweeps away the pins that are still standing and then the pin-setter comes down and sets up the next ten pins.

Could you imagine if baby teeth worked the same way? The baby wakes up one morning and, boom! Ten teeth grow in from the top of her mouth and the next morning, boom! Ten more from the bottom. I think the kid would go into shock if that happened: no one could stand the pain.

Instead, God in His mercy lets one tooth come in first, then the next and the next, minimizing the pain so that both mother and child can handle it. Besides, what would a six-month-old do with a full set of teeth anyway? Their digestive systems can't even handle hamburgers and French fries for another nine months. So God provides just enough teeth to meet a baby's growing needs.

But the kindness and the wisdom don't end there. Six years later, this same daughter comes home from first grade and says, "Look, Mommy: my tooth is loose!" That first tooth that you agonized over when she was a baby is usually the first tooth to fall out when she's a youngster. And now she's just as excited about it falling out as you were about it growing in!

And once again, what happens after that tooth? The next tooth is out, the next tooth and the next. First four in, first four out. By now, however, your six-year-old is used to eating all of the finer things in life – candy, ice cream, potato chips. What would happen if all of her teeth would've come in like bowling pins? Twenty in, twenty out. How would she eat now?

Organized replacement of one tooth at a time, so as not to interfere with the simple act of chewing – what a great act of Divine kindness! Now, you may ask: If God is so good and kind, why couldn't He just create mankind with a full set of teeth at birth (like toes and fingers that come as standard equipment) and spare everyone the pain?

Good question.

It could be that God is providing us with an invaluable lesson. A baby comes into this world and all of its needs are met. First, a protective womb nurtures the fetus until it grows to a size where it can survive in the outside world on its own systems. After birth, he has a mother to nurse him, feed him and change him; a father to encourage the mother to do these things through the night; sisters and brothers to entertain him, plug him with a pacifier and socialize him.

Any baby in his right mind would say, "Hey, I think I like this. All I have to do is open my mouth and I get anything I want. " And, in fact, many people never get beyond this stage of maturity, feeling that they want everyone else to take care of their every need.

So God says, "Hold on a minute. Life is not so simple. You're supposed to develop into a caring, adjusted, wonderful human being," and He throws baby a curve ball. One night, he wakes up with this pain in his mouth and says, "What happened? What did I do? Why am I suffering like this?" Baby doesn't have the answer. Mommy is pretty sure he's teething, but every few days she calls the doctor and asks, "Are you sure it's not a virus?"

This pain goes on for quite a while, until finally baby and mommy discover the answer. All of this suffering was so that baby can acquire his ultimate reward – a tooth! A gleaming white, magnificent tooth that he can use in ways he never before imagined. A hard lesson to learn, a tough experience to live through, and the baby doesn't even understand what just happened. But he soon discovers that the tooth was worth the trouble.

Many of us do the same thing: we go through life with all of its frustrations and miseries and we say, "Why me? Why is God treating me like this?"

We need to understand that every pain, every anxiety, every scratch on the car is really for our ultimate benefit. God will never give us a test that we can't pass, just as He wouldn't give a baby ten teeth all at once. Our job is to recognize that things don't just happen by themselves, that there is a Creator Who is watching over every detail of our lives and does things solely for our benefit. We may not always understand the challenge and many times the reward takes longer to come around than we would like. But it's important to realize that whatever happens to us comes from the source of all goodness, God Himself.

Now that our six-year-old is sixteen, I wonder if He could figure out how to lower the orthodontist's bill. That would be a *real* kindness.

THE ELIXIR

The following is a multi-part, multiple-choice question, with only one correct answer:

Question:

What expands as it contracts and contracts as it expands?

What is heavier than air and lighter than air?

What is colorless and colorful?

What is separate from me, but when I use it, becomes more than half of me?

What is tasteless, yet delicious?

What warms me up or keeps me cool?

What is the basis of all life yet can only be found in one place?

Answers:

A. Water

B. Don't know

Did you choose A? I hope so, even if it was just a guess. Few people realize the many wondrous aspects of one of the most important substances in the universe – this stuff we call water.

Let's start with the greatest thing about water: we have it and no one else does. As far as scientists can tell, this is the only place in our galaxy, and possibly in the entire universe, that has liquid water. Oh, there's plenty of H_2O out there: meteors have water (in fact, some are solid ice); Mars and Venus may have had water; but the Earth's water is unique. That's because water only exists as a liquid between 32 degrees and 212 degrees Fahrenheit. The temperature of outer space is about minus 400 degrees. Thanks to our exact positioning near the sun and the properties of the Earth's atmosphere, we have the real thing – soluble, drinkable, pure water.

So much for the big stuff. For those who like the little stuff of life like DNA, RNA and stem cells, there would be none of that, if not for water. Water is necessary for carbon to form all of the long protein strings that are the basis of life. If we didn't have it, organic life just wouldn't exist.

But let's get down to the practical stuff. If I'm hot, I can put a few pieces of frozen water in soda. If I'm cold, I boil some water and add a teabag. If I'm taking an aspirin, a glass of water has practically no taste, but if I'm really thirsty, there's nothing more delicious or satisfying than a cool glass of H_2O.

And what happens to that water when it gets inside of me? It lubricates my joints, aids in the flow of blood, helps me digest my food and becomes 65% of almost every cell of my body.

Hold up a glass of water and take a look at it. It's clear, colorless and transparent. Now take a trip to the Swiss Alps or northern Montana or Alaska. (You don't have to do it now, but let's say that you did.) Take a look at that same water, frozen by nature. It takes on a beauty and color that rivals the greenest greenery and the bluest skies.

Did you ever consider that the water that we have today has gone through hundreds of thousands of changes, yet remains as pure today as it was at the beginning of time? The system works something like this:

In the oceans it's a liquid. When the sun evaporates it and changes it to a gas, it becomes lighter than air and rises purified of all dirt, salt and chemicals, floating as a cloud. As it condenses, it becomes heavier than air once again and falls as rain. Mankind then uses it to drink, wash, digest, clean, extinguish, irrigate, swim in and travel on. Eventually it flows back to the oceans from where it came, only to rise again, cleaned and purified from all of the chemicals and contaminants. In short, water simply never gets used up. It might be redistributed, but it seems like it will always be here.

But there is still one characteristic of water that makes it different from just about everything else. Did you ever notice that ice cubes float? Of course you did. Nothing special about that, right?

Let's see.

It's a basic law of science that as objects heat up they expand, and as they cool, they contract. Just look at any poorly constructed highway. They buckle in the summer and get potholes in the winter.

Water is the same way – to a point. As it heats up to boiling, it expands and becomes a gas, taking up more and more space, becoming less dense. As it cools, it contracts, taking up less space and becoming denser. This is why the bathtub water is always cooler at the bottom (more dense, therefore heavier) and the warm water is at the top.

But then a very strange thing happens. As water cools below $39°$ Fahrenheit, instead of continuing to contract as expected, water suddenly starts to expand! By the time it freezes at $32°$, it has expanded by 10%! It's the only substance in the universe that does that!

Is that an accident of nature or a planned, necessary kindness?

Consider for a moment what would happen if water followed

nature's laws. Every winter the bottoms of lakes and rivers would freeze, killing all of their plant life, fish life and fauna. What a tragedy that would be. Instead, the frozen water rises to the top, creating a blanket of warmth for the living organisms below it by not allowing the heat from below to escape. Instead of destroying life, water actually protects life, but only because it behaves in a way that defies all scientific principles.

But why should that be so? Well, if you've begun to see the world as I do, you will answer that water has these unique qualities because the world was created as an act of kindness. If its Creator intended to provide a life of fullness, richness and beauty for its inhabitants, then natural laws that would leave the oceans barren and polluted just don't fit into the plan. So God "changed" the law in this case, just for us.

Water is the source of life, the protector of life and the elixir of life. *L'chaim!*

YOU SAID
A MOUTHFUL

You did so well on the last set of questions and answers, we're going to try it again. Only this time, the questions will get more difficult as we go on.

▸ First question: What are all of these?

Apples, bananas, oranges, cherries, plums, strawberries, peaches, pears, grapes

Answer: (1)Water (2) Fruits

If you answered (2) Fruits, you are correct. Technically, if you answered (1) Water, you are also correct. But we're still up to the easy stuff.

▸ Next question: What are all of these?
Lettuce, cabbage, green beans, potatoes, peas, carrots, cucumbers, spinach, cauliflower, asparagus, broccoli

Answer: (1)Fruits (2) Vegetables
Once again, if you answered number (2), you are correct.

▸ Here's an easy one: What are these?
Steak, hamburgers, hot dogs, veal chops, lamb chops, chicken wings, liver

Answer: (1)Meats (2) Ingredients for a great barbeque
Both are correct. Well, except for the liver, maybe.

▸ One more, then it starts to get harder. What are these?
Milk, soda, juice, wine, beer, champagne

Answer: (1) Types of drinks (2) Variations of water
Once again, both are correct.

▸ Now here's a tougher one. What do *all* of the above have in common?

Answer: (1) They're something we eat or drink (2) They're good for us (3) They add pleasure to life (4) All of the above
Even though you may not like beer, liver or broccoli, the answer is (4) All of the above.

▸ Here's the final question, but I'm not going to give you any hints. You have to come up with the answer on your own:

In one word, what is a unique characteristic that they all have in common, but is different in all of them?

Think about it; I told you it was going to be hard.

So what did you come up with? Color, shape, size? Calories, maybe? All good answers, but you could say that about almost anything. The one thing they all have in common that's different is – taste.

These tasteful pleasures of delight are sweet, sour, tart, bitter, juicy, succulent, mouth-watering, tantalizing and intoxicating.

You can add to this array of flavor such things as sugar, salt, onion, honey, cinnamon, lemon, oregano, peppermint, paprika, garlic, dill weed, parsley, sage, rosemary and thyme. And don't forget the ketchup, mustard, barbeque sauce and pickles.

But none of this would make any difference if we didn't have a way of enjoying them. Think about it. With millions of taste buds covering the upper surface of our tongues, we can enjoy the smallest nuances and hints of flavor in all of the foods that we eat. Is it any surprise that mankind has the most highly developed sense of taste of any species on Earth?

And that makes a lot of sense. After all, could you picture a monkey eating a double-chocolate-fudge-banana-split-ice-cream-sundae? No. Because he would probably just spit out the ice cream and eat the bananas. And even though they tell you that Purina Dog Chow tastes better than Alpo, how do they really know?

Complex, sensitive taste buds are reserved for mankind, as are the vast variety of foods that exist. Is this just a coincidence, or once again, do we see the benevolent design of a loving Creator Who wants us to derive constant, varied pleasure even during the necessary, daily act of eating?

We're not limited to just these hundreds of different fruits and vegetables and meats and drinks. What about the wonderful foods we make from grains such as wheat, rye, corn, spelt, oats, rice and barley?

Or some fun stuff – like potato chips, soda, ice cream and candy?

Or the staples – like fish, eggs, cheese and poultry?

Or the kid stuff – like waffles, cookies, cakes and Cocoa Pebbles?

It's a true garden of delights for man to feast upon out there! And we just happened to be equipped with the right kind of receiver, taste buds, to make sure that we don't just exist, but that we enjoy.

Anybody hungry?

THE HAND
OF GOD

Everyone has his story: A moment in time when you were sure that Divine Providence had interceded on your behalf and affected the ultimate course of your life. Whether it was the choice of a spouse, a new business venture or not getting on the plane that eventually crashed, you were sure at the time that it didn't happen by itself. Someone up there was watching out for you.

We've all had those moments. Here's mine.

Broadway, New York City: Winding its way from one end of Manhattan to the other, Broadway enjoys the reputation of being the longest street in the world. In its 12-mile stretch from the north end to the southern tip of "the City," it crisscrosses over Columbus Avenue, Amsterdam Avenue, Seventh Avenue and Fifth

Avenue. At 14th Street, it stops abruptly, only to begin again a block away.

My story takes place at West 23rd Street, where Broadway intersects with Fifth Avenue. With four separate traffic lights guiding midtown traffic through this major intersection, it's not uncommon to see cars speeding past a red light to avoid a three-minute wait for the light to change once again in their favor.

This is how I happened to be there one winter afternoon. Every day after high school, I usually stopped by my father's retail store, just a few blocks away from my school in Brooklyn. Some days, I learned the art of salesmanship, some days I lugged boxes into the storage basement, and on other days I traveled into Manhattan to pick up last-minute merchandise for the weekend customers.

This was such a day. My father gave me a list of six wholesalers to go to. Taking the subway into Manhattan, beginning at 47th Street, I made my rounds, working from uptown to downtown. I picked up camera film from one place, earrings and necklaces from another, and the newest item – refillable butane gas cigarette lighters – from another.

Laden with three heavy shopping bags, I headed for 21st Street and Fifth Avenue as my last stop before getting back on the subway.

I don't know if you've ever noticed, but New Yorkers have a strange habit (well, many strange habits, but one in particular that applies here): If they miss a light at a busy street corner, they step into the gutter and inch their way forward while the light is still red. The first ones into the street usually end up at the back of the crowd, as each newcomer steps into the empty space between two other pedestrians and moves in front of them, almost as if it were an unspoken contest to see who could get across the street first. The instant the light changes, two walls of people approach each other from opposite sides of the street.

I was also in a hurry that day, like my fellow New Yorkers. So as I approached Broadway (and Fifth) and 23rd Street, I glanced up at the light closest to me and noticed that the light had just turned red. Usually I would dash across the street before traffic started coming in the opposite direction, but since I had these heavy packages in each hand and since I was the first one at the intersection, I contented myself by merely stepping off the curb and inching my way forward as is customary in the Big Apple.

As I placed my right foot into the gutter, I felt a strong hand on my left shoulder pulling me back onto the curb. I turned around and saw a middle-aged man motioning with his head and eyes to my left. As I looked to my left, a city bus came barreling past the red light through the intersection not more than one foot away from the curb, screeching to a halt at the bus stop immediately to my right.

Had I remained in the gutter an instant longer, I would have been riding the windshield of that bus without a token. As I turned around to thank the man, he was gone. He had never said a word, but as sure as I am here today, he saved my life.

While everyone else proceeded to cross the street oblivious to what had just happened, or didn't happen, I put down my packages, took a deep breath and gave thanks to the Almighty.

My story is not unique. Close calls like that happen to thousands of people all over the globe each day. Some came to work late on that fateful day of September 11th; others decided to go to a nightclub in Tel Aviv instead of eating out on Ben Yehudah Street. There are those who sat on a crowded bus, never knowing that an alert bus driver closed the doors on a would-be terrorist and saved the lives of his innocent passengers. In a more global tragedy, there were those who were sent to the right instead of to the left and lived out the rest of their lives wondering why they had been spared while their loved ones perished.

We never know what waits for us around any corner: How many times we may have been driving next to a drunk driver and *not* gotten into an accident. How many times a thief or a murderer looked at us as their next victim, only to be pulled away by some other strange thought.

We go through life believing that we are all-powerful, invulnerable and in control – until we have *that moment*. That's when we realize that every moment is precious, that we've got to make the most of each day because we never know when that light is going to turn red.

They say that Elijah the Prophet appears here on Earth, often in the guise of an ordinary man. Maybe he appeared to me that cold December evening in Manhattan. Maybe it was an angel. Or maybe it was just some kind New Yorker, named Bill Cunningham or something, who didn't want to see a young man get flattened by a bus.

In any event, at that moment I realized with 100% clarity that I had just been given a new lease on life. Whether granted to me by God or by some guy named Bill, I have to be grateful for each day, because from that day on, it's all a gift.

THE ABC's OF KINDNESS

y now you've undoubtedly noticed that I tend to be a very positive person; that I'm thankful for just about everything in this vast, surprising world of ours. It's a habit of mine, I admit, and it's one habit worth acquiring. People who have it tend to be more optimistic and in tune with life, and they stay healthier because of it. You can make up your own list of Divine kindnesses enhancing your world – things to be personally grateful for – just as I do. Here's a list to get you started, but it's more fun to think of your own.

Aches

Nobody likes to get them, but they are the truest form of kindness. Otherwise, how would you know that your tooth was getting rotten, or that you played too many games of tennis, or that the stress at the office was beginning to take its toll on you and that it's time to slow down and rethink your priorities? Without aches, we might do irreparable damage to our bodies and not even know it.

Anger

One of many personality traits including laziness, selfishness, and kindness that can be used for good or for bad. Anger against acts of evil or injustice is good; anger about missing a traffic light is bad (and a colossal waste of energy). Working on improving our shortcomings is one of the purposes of our existence.

Animals

They were put here to provide us with labor, food, resources and companionship. They also establish a level of behavior that is normal for them, but beneath us.

Beauty

Whether it is the beauty of art, music, literature, a landscape or another's face, we have been given gifts that intrinsically bring joy to the heart. God didn't have to arrange the world this way. But He did.

Bees

Over 100,000 species of flowers rely on bees to pollinate them. If you like flowers, you can understand why we need bees. If you were a bear and liked honey, you would also understand why we need bees. Of course, if you were a bear, you would hardly understand anything.

Birth

A much more personal and interesting way of obtaining children than by buying them at Kids 'R' Us.

Cacao

To anyone who has ever craved a piece of chocolate candy, this source of cocoa is one of the greatest kindnesses.

Children

Your greatest pleasure and your greatest pain in life come from your children. They also allow you to see yourself as you truly are – forty years too late.

Desire

We all have the will to accomplish. The stronger the desire, the greater our determination to achieve our goals. When based on solid principles of right and wrong, our goals can be of the greatest benefit to the world. Based on selfishness, they lead to destruction. God gave us the free will to choose. It's all up to us.

Dew

For those of us with substantial farmland, like mine in Brooklyn, we know that we have to water our crops (especially those tomatoes) regularly or they will not grow. But for those who only have small gardens and don't have the time or inclination to take out the hose every night, there is wet stuff called dew. Due to the condensation of the water vapor in the air each night, grass, plants and cars are covered each morning with a thin layer of water that serves to irrigate the ground, without any help from us. It's just another way God keeps the world going when we're too busy to do it ourselves.

Disasters

Earthquakes, volcanoes, hurricanes and floods are among the many types of wake-up calls provided by the Creator to remind a large number of people at the same time that control of the world and its resources is beyond us.

Discovery

A Jewish seminar provided by a school called Aish HaTorah that teaches all about discovering God's kindnesses and wonders. They can be reached at (212) 921-9090. (They did not pay for this plug. I just like those folks.)

Electricity

An awesome, powerful force. It runs cities, controls our physical bodies and it is the basis of the energy of the universe. It's one of those things that can't be seen, but we know it's there because we see its effects. I think of God in this way.

Everything

There's the "Everything Bagel," the "Pizza with Everything," the "Everything for 99 Cents Store," and then there's Everything else. Everything in creation has a purpose or it wouldn't be here. One of our purposes, among many others, is to realize and actualize the potential of Everything around us, which is why we say a blessing on that bagel before we eat it.

Evil

Without darkness, we could not appreciate light. Without pain, we could not appreciate comfort. Without evil, we could not appreciate good. But the presence of evil is far more significant to us than just as a basis of comparison. Without the temptation to do evil, there would be no reward for doing good because there would be no choice! It is the free will choice of doing good rather than evil that is man's greatest challenge.

Existence

Philosopher René Descartes said, "I think, therefore I am." (Does that mean that since my secretary doesn't think, therefore, she isn't? Then why am I paying her?) He had the right idea but the wrong pronoun. Jewish philosophers maintain that we exist in the mind of God in much the same way that an author of a book conceives and sustains the lives of his characters. To remain in the script, it's advisable to have a personal relationship with the Author and make sure that we are important characters to Him in the flow of history. Descartes, therefore, should have said, "*He* thinks, therefore I am."

Fire

Like so many other elements of existence, fire can be used for good or for evil. Fire heats our homes, cooks our meals, runs our cars and lights up the night. It also consumes cities, devours forests and destroys lives. We are constantly given choices as to how we want to use the resources provided to us by the Creator. Our job is to follow His example and build, not break down.

Fluorine

A gas, a poisonous gas has been added to our drinking supply! And it's been done intentionally by the Health Department! Isn't that frightening? Fortunately, they've combined it with oxygen first, so it's no longer harmful and as a second benefit, it's also good for our teeth. From where did we get all of these crazy chemicals?

Foxhole

It must be one of the holiest places on Earth since it's the one place you'll never find an atheist.

Grandchildren

The reward that God gives you for not killing your kids during their "terrible two's" or adolescence.

Grandparents

Human beings are the only creatures that recognize family relationships beyond one generation. Grandparents also provide much-needed nurturing to a child, especially during their "terrible two's" and adolescence.

Gravity

What is this mysterious force that tethers the Earth to the sun, the moon to the Earth and you to your chair? Scientists have been trying to understand how gravity works for thousands of years. Not only that – imagine trying to play a game of tennis without it.

Health

98% of our days are spent in good health. 1% of the time we feel like we're never going to feel better, and the last 1% we regret all of the things we should have done when we were healthy. Maintaining our health is our responsibility. It's one of those gifts we have to guard like we guard our soul.

Heaven

Even though Heaven is a place of ultimate pleasure without pain, strife or suffering, most people are not in any rush to get there. Remember, though, to get into Heaven, you have to be good and late.

Home

How fortunate we are to be living in a time where we can come home to a place that offers us warmth, love, contentment, family, friends and security. This has not always been the case, as history will attest. Contained in and around our home, is *everything* we need to be thankful for.

Ideas

If anyone ever tells you, "I just got an idea," ask him from where he got it. How ideas are formed and retained has remained an enigma. Do they originate in the brain, or in a separate entity we call our mind? I have no idea.

Income tax

I'm sure there's a kindness here, but it escapes me at the moment.

In-laws

See Income Tax.

Innovations

Just think of all the things mankind has fashioned out of the materials at hand. Here are a few of my favorites.

In the home:

Microwave ovens, dishwashers, the snooze alarm, hugs, toothpaste, nail clippers, scissors, matches (the ones made in China *or* in Heaven), umbrellas, non-slip bath mats, maids, pajamas, forks, knives and spoons (especially if they match), allowance, toilet paper, paper plates, disposable diapers, toys, screen doors, dollar bills, remote control, dictionaries, rocking chairs and Sweet 'n' Low.

In the office:

White-out, paper clips, cell phones (blessing or curse, you decide), micro-chips, speaker phones, calculators, calendars, post-it memos, retirement, commuter trains and buses, yellow highlighters and weekends.

Instinct

There are very few things that babies know how to do when they are born. Fortunately, they are created with the instinct to suck, and for a while, this is their sole means of survival. Similarly, animals are also born with instincts that help them survive. But that is where the comparison ends, for animals are limited to what their instincts dictate, while Man eventually learns to utilize his instincts to help him grow, and eventually be guided by his intellect and conscience.

Joy

Our world could have been an eternally somber, serious place. But we were endowed with the ability to feel joy and a million things that could provide it.

Junk food

See Evil. Without junk food, we wouldn't appreciate the real thing.

Justice

The evildoer must be punished and the injured party compensated! That is the strict meaning of justice. Yet very few of us would like to be subject to strict justice: our reply is usually, "Officer, it wasn't my fault!" There are always extenuating circumstances that we would want the judge to consider. Fortunately, God tempers His judgment of us with mercy, without which no one would be able to survive.

Knowledge

When I was a youngster, my mother used to tell me, "Don't touch the oven; you'll burn yourself." Sound advice. I understood the wisdom of it. But it wasn't until I actually touched the oven that I "knew" exactly what she meant. In Jewish lore, knowledge represents the highest of the three levels of wisdom. It's the physical, internal realization that something is true. That is the level at which we are commanded to "know" our Creator.

Laughter

Clinically proven to add many happy years to your ...

Life

Your money or your life? Your brother or your life? Your freedom or your life? It's important to know what you are willing to die for in order to know what you should be living for. It is the only gift that matters, for without Life there is nothing. It would be a crime to waste it in pursuit of nonsense.

Love

In chronological order: Yourself, your mother, your father, your siblings, your friends, your spouse, your first child, your second child (Where does all this love come from?), your third child, your son-in-law, your first grandchild (Is it possible that there is still more love to go around?), all of your grandchildren, your spouse even more, your life.

Magnetism

Protons are positively charged particles. Electrons are negatively charged particles. Neutrons have no magnetic charges. Opposite charges attract. Without magnetism, there would be no atoms. Without atoms, there would be no physical universe. And you thought that all we needed magnetism for was for that little red horseshoe-magnet-and-nail-trick.

Marriage

Marriage has many purposes. (See Children, Parents, Grandchildren, Grandparents, Laughter and Love). But the main purpose of marriage is to bring two people together in order to perfect each of their characters. Only through the constant rubbing together of two diverse personalities can we ever hope to smooth out all of our rough edges and become a polished personality. (See also Aches, In-laws and Tuition.)

Mosquitoes

The greatest kindness would have been if Noah would have swatted the two of them when he had the chance, so we wouldn't have to hear them buzzing in our ears at 3:00 o'clock in the morning. But just as God has been kind to us, He has also been kind to the mosquito. Did you know that by the time you feel the sting of its bite, it's already long gone? That's because the pointed stinger is like a stack of ice cream cones. They collapse as they go into your skin, so you don't feel the insertion, but they open and flatten as the stinger is pulled out. This prevents us from squishing the buggers, as we'd desperately like to do, but it also allows the species to survive another day. Beats me why God would give this sophisticated escape mechanism to such an annoying creature, but then again I can't explain why He helps me out either.

Nothingness

It is just as difficult for us to envision nothingness as it is for us to understand what lies on the other end of the universe. Some believe that at the end of our days on earth we go to nothingness – a cold, sobering thought that renders this life meaningless. As difficult as it is for us to picture nothingness, it's a lot more difficult to believe that we are here for nothing.

Obstacles

Those obstacles that stand in our way of progressing perhaps benefit us the most. Overcoming them leads to the highest level of self-esteem and helps us to actualize the spiritual component of our being. If we can succeed despite a nagging spouse, an abusive boss or a physical handicap, we are that much better for having tried and succeeded. (Not that my wife nags, or anything.)

Parents

One of the greatest kindnesses is that we are born to parents, usually two. If for no other reason than that they changed your diaper for you when you couldn't do it yourself, they deserve your respect.

Peace

Of all of the necessities of life, there is little more critical than peace, for without it we are not free to enjoy all of the glorious bounty around us. On a global scale, we need peace between nations and between races. On a personal level, peace between neighbors and between husband and wife makes life worthwhile. Then there is inner peace – when we are spiritually developed enough to be content with our lives and at peace with our Creator. Of course, peace on any level cannot exist in a vacuum. We need all of them for the others to thrive.

Penicillin

It provides us with one of life's great lessons: if they can make a wonder drug out of moldy bread, than you can certainly make something out of yourself.

Pleasure

There are many different types and levels of pleasure: physical, emotional, creative and spiritual. We have the opportunity to enjoy any and all of them, however, some choose to focus only on those that are most easily attained. Yet as an athlete training for an Olympic Gold Medal knows, the greater the effort, the greater the reward.

Punishment

How many times have you said (or heard), "This is going to hurt me more than it hurts you"? Inflicting punishment is never an easy thing to do – especially to someone you love. But as every parent knows, sometimes punishments are necessary: They are an indication to the person that he was doing something unacceptable. Done properly, with the result that the person mends his ways, it can be a great kindness and benefit, even though it hurts.

Q

A heavy hitter in any game of Scrabble, Q reminds us to bide our time and wait for opportunities to make the best use of our assets. Don't squander your valuable assets on every silly little quest, but when you have the chance to discover the quintessential truths of the universe, that's the time to make your move.

Quality

Quality of life has become a very big issue in many cities – clean streets, less crime, free-flowing traffic. (Well, maybe that's a little too much to ask.) Quality in products is also an issue, as consumers demand more value for their money. Quality time with children is coming to the forefront as more and more couples are finding themselves working longer hours to make ends meet. It's a tribute to mankind that we care about quality, as well as a reminder that God cares about quality too. If He put us here, we must have what it takes to fulfill the purpose He intended. Human beings are a high-quality product.

Quiet

Those moments in the day after all of the other workers have gone home, after the kids have gone to sleep, after the TV and radio are off, when you can stop and consider where you are, what you've accomplished and where you are going.

Radioactivity

There are elements out there that are radioactive. They are chemically unstable and will disintegrate over a period of time.

So? What does that have to do with us? These elements are now the basis for nuclear energy, the energy of the future. God exists outside of time, so for Him there is no past, present or future. So when He created the world, it was all present tense for Him. But knowing the future, He had to include all of the things that we would need thousands of years later. Fortunately for us, radioactivity was one of those things. Because from our perspective, the future is now.

Saturday

I have several daughters living at home. Therefore, we have three phone lines, two cell phones, four extensions and two long-distance carriers. In my house, the phones never stop ringing, even on Saturday. The only difference is, on Saturdays nobody answers them. It's a day of peace, quiet and tranquility, 52 times a year. It's called Shabbat. It doesn't get better than this.

Smells

One of the sensual pleasures that also didn't have to be, but is. Smells can be subtle, serene, offensive, alluring, breathtaking, invigorating or noxious. They can be powerful in numerous ways, even evoking a memory of where you experienced that smell before, more vividly than any visual image can. They also add to our pleasure of eating and actually trigger the digestive process to begin before we even take the first bite. Smells are the closest thing to a physical-spiritual pleasure that we can get.

Tuna

A delicious food, so versatile you can eat it in a hero sandwich, splash it on a salad or bake it in the oven. In an emergency, you can even enjoy it straight out of the can. Precious as it is, it is still a fish so abundant that it is relatively inexpensive and available nearly everywhere in the world. Which is lucky for me, because I believe that I hold the world's record for eating the most tuna fish sandwiches in one lifetime!

Transfusions

Blood transfusions have been taking place for almost a hundred years. Medical science has made enormous progress in transplanting organs such as hearts, livers, kidneys and soon, brains. Why should this be possible? Why should the organs of one person work in the body of another? Every human being is different, yet the basic components have been standardized in order to preserve and prolong human life. Of course, this possibility raises the question, "Why prolong life?" What is it for? Why are we here?

Tuition

See Income tax.

USA

You'll excuse me if I'm a little bit prejudiced, but I think that America is one of the miracles of Creation. It stands for all of the highest principles of equality and justice, even though it may not always get it right, and it is probably the greatest country in the history of the world.

Variety

We could eat plain bread and drink water every day. And all of our clothes could be white. And all flowers could be red. And everyone could own the same kind of car, live in the same type of house and play the same board game every night (probably Monopoly). And there could be one kind of animal in the zoo and only one instrument to play and all faces could look alike. But, thank God, there's variety.

Weather

It gives total strangers something to talk about. It provides variety. It gives us something to look forward to, four times a year. It makes us appreciate what a 23-degree tilt in the world's axis can do.

Who/What/Where/When/Why?

The inquisitive nature of man (not to mention nosy journalists) causes him to ask these questions. The drive to find the answers helps man change the world, hopefully for the better.

X-rays

A form of energy with a high frequency and short wave length. The shorter the wave length, the more the energy waves are able to pierce solid objects, as radio-waves do. X-rays also have the ability to expose filament and leave an image. It helps doctors diagnose broken bones, tumors, and cavities. Modern medical science would never be where it is now without this early form of noninvasive exploration.

Yeast

First and foremost, yeast is a fungus. If we left it at that, we would never be able to change matzoh into bread, brownies into cake or hops into beer. How fortunate we are that we discovered its true purpose and learned how to use yucky to create yummy.

Zygote

The beginning of *you*. This world of beauty, kindness, wonder, perfection, symmetry and unity was all placed here for you to use, explore and enjoy. But it wouldn't mean anything to you if *you* weren't here. But you are. And that's where your journey begins.

Body
and Soul

TWIN BRIDGES

√

What would happen if kids could talk? Not just 2-year-olds or 3-year-olds, but as soon as they came out of the womb. Imagine if they had a full vocabulary. Then, instead of crying at all hours of the night, you could talk to them intelligently and explain why they should spend the next eight hours sleeping instead of screaming.

If babies could talk, most parents would probably like to ask, "Why were you always jumping around like that? And, could you really tell when mommy ate asparagus and when she ate chocolate cake?"

But a far more important question would be, "What did you think would happen to you after you left the womb?" You might be very surprised at the answer.

Let's imagine we could listen in on a conversation between a set of twins who are just about to be born. It might sound something like this:

"So?"

"So what?"

"So what do you think is going to happen to us?"

"When?"

"Now. There's no more room in here for us. Excuse me, please get your foot out of my ear again."

"Oh, sorry."

"What do you think happens to us after this?"

"Well, we'll probably get out of here and go to a much bigger world where there's room for both of us."

"What are you talking about? What other world? There's no place else outside of this balloon."

"I don't know. I feel like there has to be another existence after this one."

"And why do you say that?"

"Well, the way I look at it, if we had both started off in here fully grown and little by little we started shrinking, I'd agree with you that we'd probably just disappear one day. But we didn't. We started off small and now we're getting bigger and bigger. Remember when I used to make fun of you 'cause you looked like a fish and I looked like a rabbit? Look at you now. You've got these big strong muscles and bright red hair. You'll probably grow up to be a football player or something."

"Yeah, and what about you?"

"Me? I hate football. Maybe I'll be a teacher or a professor."

"I'm telling you, you're crazy. There is nothing outside of this place. Once we're finished here, it's all over. We're both gonna die."

And so, their conversation goes on for the next few days until, suddenly, the walls start shaking.

"This is it, kid. We're outta here. Been nice knowing you."

"Don't worry. There's more to life than this. I can feel it in my bones."

"You're feeling my bones again."

"Oh, sorry."

When a tunnel begins to open, the "thinker" disappears from his brother's view, but his voice can still be heard: "See you in the next world!"

When he emerges from the tunnel, he is overjoyed! He looks at his new surroundings and lets out a scream of excitement. But, alas, instead of saying, "Hello, world, here I am!" it comes out, "Whaaaaa."

Still inside the womb, his brother hears this scream, shrugs his tiny shoulders and says to himself, "I knew I was right. My brother is dead!" He feels an indescribable sadness.

A few moments later, he too is pushed through the same tunnel. He thinks he knows what's waiting for him, so he allows himself to be pushed along slowly, not in any rush to get to his final destination. Suddenly, he is in a world of bright light, with delightful sensations and happy voices heartily exclaiming, "Congratulations, it's another boy!"

And soon he finds himself under a deliciously warm light, next to his brother, in a huge world that seems without limit.

The same way that an infant in the womb cannot picture an outside world, we too cannot fathom what a Next World would look like.

Now nobody likes talking about death, but there's no getting away from the fact that sooner or later, everyone has to die. It's just that most of us would like to ignore this certainty for most of our lives. Imagine you go to a funeral and the speaker says, "Dearly beloved, we are gathered here today to mourn the passing of Jane, a fine woman who always looked great, dressed beautifully and had a mean tennis serve. She will be best remembered by her closest friend Theresa for that time she voluntarily took her own manicure money and paid Theresa's parking ticket without her knowing it. Jane is survived by her pet cat, a one-bedroom apartment on the East side and an extensive wardrobe."

Poor Jane! If she had only known she was going to die, she might have wanted to give people a few more nice things to say about her at her funeral.

All things being equal, someone will be called upon to say a few nice things about us too. What would we want them to say?

(And here we can be a little selfish.) We would probably like them to say the most noble things possible. Luckily, we have a lifetime to prepare them. We can decide today how we would like to be remembered and start working on ourselves from now on.

The person who believes that this world is all that there is believes he is going from meaningless to nothingness. But just as surely as we know that birth is a bridge that leads to life and to this world (because we experience it all around us), we will eventually understand that death too is a bridge that leads to an even more glorious life in another dimension.

And just as a baby begins from a microscopic drop and develops its physical structure while in the womb in order to be able to survive in this physical world, human beings are born with a pure, innocent soul that is meant to be developed and nurtured while we are in this world – to prepare it for eternal life in the World to Come.

PLUMBING

I don't know if you remember, but several years ago the city of Cleveland was on the verge of bankruptcy. It had run out of money and was about to shut down all services. It has since rebounded and today is a very prosperous, growing city.

At about the time Cleveland was having fiscal problems, a huge condominium complex was being built downtown, in an effort to attract young professionals back to Cleveland. The buildings needed to be completed, otherwise they'd be an embarrassment and the city would be stuck with these white elephants forever.

One of the architects came up with an idea. If they skimped on some of the building code requirements, they could get away cheaper. (I think he's in jail somewhere now.) One of his ideas was to use only one set of pipes to bring in fresh water and to take out the wastewater. He would try to work out the water pressure system so that the fresh water would be forced into the faucets and then all the waste would drain out of the same pipes.

Could you imagine such a thing? One set of pipes for clean and dirty? Who would want to live there?

Actually, we all live there. No, not in Cleveland, but in ourselves.

We have a circulatory system. It carries food, nutrients and fresh oxygen to every cell in our body. It drops off the good clean stuff, and then picks up the waste material from every cell and continues on its way. One set of pipes, thirty trillion cells.

What would life be like if our bodies didn't have the capabilities of extracting these nutrients from the food we eat? Food itself would be deadly poison if it entered the bloodstream as it is. Imagine having hot chili sauce coursing through your veins.

So the digestive system, with its intricate coordination of breaking down food, beginning with the saliva in our mouths, to the acids of our stomachs, to the bile of the liver, to the hundred-foot-long intestines, prepares food for absorption into the bloodstream.

The blood then latches onto these nutrients and brings them to each area of our bodies – specific components for each type of body part. Our bones, muscles, nerves, skin and immune systems all need different types of nourishment. And somehow the blood system figures out how to deliver each one to the exact location without fail, on time, every second of the day.

Who taught the blood how to do that? How *does* it do that? How does it know what nutrient to take to which cell? Does DNA, which is nothing more then electrons, protons, and neutrons, keep a delivery tally at the exit of your heart, and say, "Ok, you go here, and you go there"?

How marvelous is this organism called the human body.

Did you ever stop and think about your kidneys? That's okay, most people don't. They filter about 1,000 pounds of blood every day, removing all the waste material and eliminating it from the body through the urine.

When was the last time you changed the filter in your kidneys? In your car you have to change it every 3,000 miles. How come you don't have to change anything in your kidneys?

Speaking of cars, when they're running low on gas, the "Low Fuel" indicator lights up. When *we're* running low on fuel, the sensation of hunger takes over and we know it's time to refuel. In a car, when it's low on water, the engine's temperature gauge moves to "Hot." Humans just realize they're thirsty and gladly shell out a buck and a half for a cold bottle of soda.

And speaking of temperature gauges, did you know that even when the thermometer says your body temperature is 98.6°, you have organs that are normally hotter and others that are normally colder. The body automatically self-regulates both the temperature and the blood pressure of every organ individually.

To do this, the body has a system of glands that secrete hormones that have to be perfectly measured, or the organ and the body cease to function. The thyroid, for example, which regulates blood calcium, heart rate and digestion, produces only one teaspoonful of thyroxine per year and it has to be released in exact measured doses. And for most people for most of their lives, that is done *perfectly.*

Ever have to fix your car and you didn't have the right tool? You know what substitutes for pliers, hammers and screwdrivers? Our hands! And they're are also capable of writing, sewing, drawing, soothing, scratching, and expressing our innermost, animated thoughts (especially if you're Jewish). Our hands are more highly developed than those of any other living creature and are the most marvelous and versatile of all our features.

This wondrous machine, our body, has been entrusted to us for 80, 90, or 100 years, to enjoy the pleasures of this world, to help make the world a better place and to use in the service of God.

And just as it says in that last clause on a typical car lease, we've got to return it back to the Original Manufacturer in good condition, except for normal wear and tear.

TELEPHONE
TAG

Here are a few Great Moments in History, for old times' sake:

March 1875. In a small town in Massachusetts, a young inventor picks up his latest invention and shouts to his assistant in the next room, "Watson, come here; I want you." Alexander Graham Bell has just completed the first telephone call in history. What began as an idea has since become a revolution (not to mention a pile of bills).

December 7, 1941. The Japanese have just attacked Pearl Harbor. President Franklin Delano Roosevelt characterizes the day in a speech to Congress as "a date which will live in infamy." The United States enters the war and, through the righteous might and perseverance of the American people, wins absolute victory.

July 19, 1969. Neil Armstrong utters the words that will shake the world: "That's one small step for man, a giant leap for mankind." The *New York Times* reports the next day, "Man Walks on the Moon." Truly one of man's greatest scientific achievements.

May 12, 2001. Your son Michael's neutrophils and macrophages announce, "Send in the phagocytes! There has been an invasion of microorganisms into the fifth portside digit."

Now, you may have a faint recollection of one or two of these Great Moments, but what's going on with Michael? First let's translate into the vernacular. What the message means is, "Mommy, I got a cut on my finger!"(if Michael were doing the talking). What's with these neutrophils and macrophages?

They are actually antibodies that live inside of you and me and they are just one part of the wondrous communication system of the body. In my opinion, its daily activities are far more critical and infinitely more astounding than all of man's successes and achievements in the worlds of science, politics and economics.

Now, let's say that you ask your little Michael, "Son, how did you hurt yourself?" He might reply, " I saw Billy's dog running after me and I got scared, so I ran away and I fell."

If Michael were really, really perceptive (more like your side of the family), he would have noted that his eyes had sent a signal to his brain, his brain then sent a message to his adrenal glands and they immediately responded by secreting more sugar into his bloodstream to give him a burst of energy so he could run away, and more clotting agent to prepare his body for scrapes. In fact, he just saw Billy's dog coming after him and the rest was done automatically by his body.

So now you gently wash the dirt off his cut, bandage it snugly and give it a kiss. He looks up lovingly at you and says, "Thank you, Mommy." You take one more look at it and think, maybe the bandage is too tight. So you ask, "Can you still move your little finger?"

He says, "Sure." Within an instant, Michael's inner mechanisms take over once again. His brain sends a stream of electric impulses flowing through his nerves, past the synapses, into his arm, through his hand and into his finger. Before you can blink an eye, he wiggles his pinky. Another hidden communication, right before your very eyes, with no strings attached.

But let's get back to the phagocytes.

Now, I'm a big boy and I don't cry. And you better believe that if I scrape my finger, there's no way I'm going to go blabbing about it to all my friends, relatives and acquaintances. But that's exactly what the body does.

There are over thirty trillion cells in an adult human body and if anything goes wrong in any area of the entire organism, every cell hears about it. Some don't do anything more than just sympathize, like my friends would do, but some components, like phagocytes, are actually dispatched from every area of the body to fight off invading germs, bacteria and microbes.

So let's get back to Michael. There go his phagocytes, speeding through an intricate maze of blood vessels and body tissue to seek, destroy and devour anything that might cause harm to his body. They can even distinguish between types of organisms with an almost intelligent understanding of who the good guy is (Michael) and who the bad guys are (germs).

Phagocytes don't operate alone to protect his body – there's an entire army in there. For example, what would have happened if Michael's cut were really nasty and had started bleeding? The body's bone marrow would have immediately been alerted to start producing new red blood cells, even as much as ten times the normal amount. When the level had normalized, the all-clear signal would have gone out and the bone marrow would return to its regular level of production.

Now let's ask an even more obvious question. How can submicroscopic cell parts communicate? And with over 100,000 enzyme particles in every cell, how does the body pick out the correct ones to call on? And not just from one or two cells, but from trillions of them. Even my daughters don't make that many calls! And not only from *adjacent* cells, we are talking about coordinating functions and priorities over vast distances, at least in terms of cell size, simultaneously. It's sort of like playing "telephone" on a global scale.

And that's just to fight off microbes. There's also the constant flow of involuntary instructions from the brain to breathe, pump, blink and digest. That's in addition to the voluntary instructions to walk, run, sit, stand, push, pull, chew, talk and smile.

The common answer to this question is DNA: the computer program that's installed in every living organism. It's fully coded into every cell of our bodies and contains the formula to reproduce and repair every other cell. When something needs to be done, DNA makes the call. The only question is – which part of the atom does the dialing?

The electrons, because they're already running around in circles anyway?

The protons, because they're on the inside and always know what's going on?

Or maybe the neutrons, because they're neutral and they don't care *who* gets the credit?

If DNA is the software and the human cell is the hardware, then there must be a Programmer. Who is it? Who gives intelligence to these sub-atomic particles to intelligently communicate over long distances to everyone in the neighborhood all at one time?

It isn't Michael. It isn't you. Have I mentioned before that I think it's God?

Call Him and ask.

CLOTHES MAKE THE MAN

Comedienne Carol Burnett used to tell of when she went to her 25th high school reunion and saw one of her friends whom she hadn't seen since the old days. The only reason she was able to recognize her was that the lady was wearing the same dress that she used to wear twenty-five years ago!

So many of us underestimate the tremendous benefits we get from clothing. It keeps us warm. It keeps us cool. It covers us up and it shows us off. It hides us from embarrassment and it feeds our egos. It also separates us from the animals because we are the only species on Earth that uses clothing, except of course for some French poodles on New York's Upper West Side.

How lucky we are to be living in an age where we have so many more options to choose from beyond bear hides, lamb-skins and fig leaves. Not only that, but imagine if you lived thousands of years ago before anyone knew how to shear a lamb, comb its hair, spin it and weave it into wool; or before anyone realized the tremendous potential of the cotton plant. You just wouldn't bother getting out of bed in the morning. What would you wear?

Probably just your skin, like the people in the South of France or the Isles of Tahiti. Although, technically, skin doesn't qualify as clothing, it does cover our bodies completely. It's also more durable than cotton, easier to clean than polyester and more miraculous than Velcro.

Did you know that one square inch of skin contains four million cells, four feet of blood vessels, five yards of nerves and one hundred and twenty sweat glands? And not only does it continue to grow as we do, it also expands and contracts almost instantaneously, as needed – like in our cheeks when we bite off more than we can chew, or on our elbows and knees when we exercise and around our bellies when we are expecting a baby (or eating a big meal).

It also blushes when we get embarrassed, whitens when we get frightened and tans beautifully when we visit the South of France or Tahiti. No animal skin can do that.

Speaking of animals, how come an animal that lives in the wild, or works hard on a farm or prowls in a back alley somewhere, gets only one set of clothing, while mankind has housing with climate control and can constantly replace clothing? For animals, what they're born with is what they get (though if I were a peacock or a mink, I wouldn't complain). But we can always go to Macy's or Walmart whenever we want; they're always running some kind of sale.

And clothing nowadays is so practical. Take the belt, for instance. It holds up your pants or your skirt. It tucks in your stomach. It's made from leather for flexibility with a sturdy metal buckle to make it durable. It has several holes in it – one for before lunch and one for after lunch.

While I can understand belts, I never understood neckties. Remember not so long ago, when men used to wear ties, even on Fridays? Now don't get me wrong, I love ties, but what do we need them for? Legend has it that it started as a piece of chain mail worn by knights around their necks for protection. In order to look really macho, the knight wore it even when not in battle, to show that he was always ready for a fight. (As for me, I could think of better ways to look macho without choking myself.) Then the Italians took over and started making them out of silk, charging us $35 apiece for a closet full of fashion statements.

While clothing certainly is important to us, but not as important as air or water, how long do you think you can go without buying a new set of clothes? Now, I'm not referring to shoes, because as every husband knows a woman must have a new pair of shoes every other week. But consider clothing. How long can a person go before s/he needs a new wardrobe? Four months, six months? For men, it's much longer. (Some of my outfits are older than my kids!)

In general, most people will buy various articles of clothing throughout the year. Of course, clothing itself doesn't grow naturally. So it would seem that whoever put together the world with all of the cotton plants, flax, animal hides, wool and polyester chemicals did it all for the benefit of mankind alone.

What a tremendous kindness that these components for making man's clothing are available in such abundance. What a greater kindness it is that we have the wisdom to know how to use them.

OUT OF
THE MOUTHS
OF BABES

The battle rages on:
"He said me first."
"No, he said *me* first."
"No, he didn't, he said me first!"
So what *was* your baby's first word?

Sorry, Dad, but usually it's "ma-ma." Why? Is it because baby likes Mommy more than he likes you? Is he a Momma's boy? Should you have spent less time at the office?

The answer is probably none of the above. Ma-ma is simply one of the easiest sounds for a baby to make, besides crying.

Infants are constantly exploring the world of sounds. But even after a baby has learned to make the right sounds, it usually takes several months more until he can even imagine that there's a meaning to them. By the time the average baby is eighteen months old, he will know how to say more than 100 words and know, more or less, the meaning of each one. (And Grandma will say he's brilliant.)

So what does a baby need in order to go about learning how to speak?

Let's pretend for a moment that you are a baby. There you are, lying in your crib, and you start cooing. Wow! Everyone laughs and smiles when you do it, and you get that warm, fuzzy feeling all over.

So the first thing you need is encouragement.

Next you learn how to click your tongue, smack your lips and gurgle. But that doesn't make words. For that, you need a voice box.

Wow! How lucky you are – you have one of those!

Now what you need to do is learn to articulate sounds with your lips, your tongue, your palate and your throat.

Great! You've got those too and you put them to use. Now here comes the hard part. Through experience, you have to learn what these semi-intelligent sounds mean. For example:

UP means – Mommy, I want you to hold me.

MAW means – I'm not finished yet; give me another portion.

NO means – I *am* finished; *don't* give me MAW.

And then you need a general agreement with everyone around you as to what these words mean to them. You put all of these things together and life is better than you ever imagined it could be: until now, you always thought that you were going to have to go through the rest of your life crying in order to get what you want. And let's face it, how far do you think you can go in the world if all you know how to do is whine? Yeah, well, you're right, you could become just about anything.

Okay, now pretend that you're a grown-up again.

What an awesome concept, this idea of speech! It gives us the ability to communicate. It elevates us above the level of animals. It allows us to convey our thoughts, our knowledge and emotions in words that can be understood. And not only words help us communicate, but also volume, pitch, inflection and emphasis (not to mention hand motions).

Also, if you have the time to learn them, you can say the same thing in over sixty-eight hundred languages and, if you look hard enough, you might actually find people who could understand you!

Without speech, social relationships between people would be impossible. It is only through this gift of speech that man can give expression to what is in his mind and understand the soul of another human being. Why wasn't this gift given to every other living creature? Surely, other species have their own means of communicating, but none with the clarity and sophistication that has been afforded to mankind. Even monkeys and dolphins, that have the ability to recognize and use what we consider words, don't have the ability to express new ideas. They can only repeat what they've learned or what they know instinctively.

Ultimately, what man needs in order to speak is a spiritual ability, an intelligence that transcends the bodily features of vocal cords, teeth and tongue. We see that animals have these physical features too, yet they can't speak.

According to the Bible, when God "breathed" the breath of life into Adam's nostrils, Adam became a living being. Living means socializing, understanding, communicating, articulating. It is no coincidence that historians and sociologists established that recorded history began 6,000 years ago. (Okay, so they're off by 250 years.)

Speech is just one of the spiritual abilities that God has given to man to allow us to utilize our superior intellect, hopefully to do good things. Highly spiritual people know that when they use the gift of speech it should be to speak to others about worthwhile ideals and concepts, not just idle chatter about people and events.

So even when you feel like babbling like a baby, don't forget to pretend that you're a grown-up.

FORGET ME NOT

We all know what oxymorons are – expressions that contradict themselves: like "military intelligence" or "rap music" or "exact estimate."

But what would you say about a purple orange?

Well, maybe it's not an oxymoron, but it's certainly not something that you see every day.

What would happen if, twenty years from now, someone served you a dish of fruit, and there in the middle of the cantaloupes and pineapples was a purple orange? Which would surprise you more, the fact that they actually came up with a purple orange or that you remembered hearing about this exotic fruit twenty years earlier?

The way that science is progressing nowadays, it should come as no surprise if somebody figures out how to combine blueberries and beets with an orange and produces something purple that tastes like an orange. But how is it that just by reading about it today, an image can be fixed in your mind and remain a memory that stays part of your sub-conscious for twenty years – and then, when you're served this phenomenal new fruit, it triggers the memory in your mind and brings it back to you in living color?

What is this wonder called memory?

By reading, hearing, seeing or sensing something, it becomes an actual, physical reality within the gray matter of your brain. Scientists don't know exactly how it works (surprise, surprise), but they do know that everything that a person experiences in his lifetime is recorded permanently in the brain. From your earliest childhood moments, to the day you graduated high school, to the face of a passerby in the street, everything is there to be recalled.

And while there are those who can recall every New York Yankee batting average back to the 1921 World Series, there are those who worry about clogging up their heads with useless information (not that batting averages aren't important). Albert Einstein, a guy who knew a few things about a few things, is said to have used only 15% of his total brain capacity. So it seems that the storage of memories is almost endless!

What would a human being be without the ability to remember? First of all, he would never know where he lived or what he owned. He wouldn't know who he should be nice to because he could never remember who are his friends and who are his enemies. He couldn't sing the words of his favorite song and he would never remember what time the Seven o'clock News started no matter how many times you told him.

We would say that such a person is totally divested of one of the most basic qualities that make up a human being. Memory gives us the ability to make intelligent decisions based upon the implications of those memories, known as experience. It differentiates us from the beasts of the field who act primarily out of instinct and whose daily decisions revolve around, "Should I eat grass, or should I eat grass?"

It's a good thing that we have the ability to remember!

The converse of this also has serious consequences. What if a person could never forget? Such a person could never be happy because he would always be dwelling on all of the terrible things that happened to him in his life. First of all, he would never forgive his mother for all the pain she put him through during childbirth. His mother would also be a little miffed at all the pain he put *her* through during childbirth. He would remember every slight, every hurt, every time his boss gave him a nasty look, every time his wife said his tie didn't match his suit. In short, he would be miserable!

You know how sometimes you say, "I just can't get that song out of my head"? Imagine if you couldn't forget it for thirty years!

It's a good thing that we have the ability to forget! (Did I just say that? Oh, no.) Because, in fact, there are terrible things that happen to us, like losing a job or missing the lottery number by one digit. Some things can stop us in our tracks and prevent us from enjoying all of the other pleasures that life has to offer. But thanks to the fading away of these memories into our subconscious, we are able to forget and to get on with our lives.

Remembering, forgetting, speech, shame and kindliness are all part of the spiritual aspects of our beings that elevate us above all other creatures. They've been given to us to promote the general welfare of all mankind, not just for ourselves as individuals.

I just wonder if it will have pits. "If what will have pits?" I hear you ask.

The purple orange. You forgot already?

WHEN ALL ELSE FAILS

Forget for a moment that the Bible, the Five Books of Moses, has been the guiding light of the Jewish people for over 3,000 years. And forget that it has been adopted by two other religions of the world with almost 3 billion believers.

While the Bible could be viewed as just a collection of stories, it's considerably more than that. In fact, it is a book that has changed the world both on a global scale and for individuals. If you go back far enough, you will see that all societies were polytheistic, believing in a multiplicity of imperfect gods. Along comes Abraham (You can find him in the Bible.) who says that there is only one God. What's more, He is a caring, benevolent Creator of all humanity. He didn't just create the world and go on vacation. He knows about us and wants us to get to know about Him. Throughout the Bible, He sets an example for all humanity to follow through numerous loving acts of kindness.

Before the nations of the world made the quantum leap of forsaking their own religions for the God of the Jewish Bible, people used to do nasty things like kill others for population control, for recreation or to appease a jealous god. Abraham (in the Bible, remember?) comes along and says that murder is wrong and that every life is infinitely valuable. Says God told him so. Later on, this Divine document adds some laws commanding people to love one another, to pursue justice, to help the less fortunate, to view everyone as equal before the law and to establish a just leadership.

And pretty soon, people buy into it – by the billions. So much so that the Bible has since formed the basis of modern democracies around the world. Our own Founding Fathers relied heavily on the Bible for determining how to best establish a moral and just society. The Declaration of Independence is a powerful testimony to the greatness and importance of the Bible by its recognition of the most fundamental truth that "All men are created equal and are endowed by their Creator with the right to life, liberty and the pursuit of happiness." The Bible and its idea of one God, more than anything else in the history of the world, have changed the world for the better.

And while the Bible carries myriad messages, there are two that we need to focus on for our purposes.

Number one: what would happen if I gave you a wristwatch as a present? Chances are you would look at it and say thank you. But what if I told you that it was 14-karat gold, 17-jewel, shockproof and waterproof; you could also use it as a calendar, a calculator, a Palm Pilot, a cell phone and you could get your email messages on it? Chances are you would be more impressed with it and would be more grateful than if you thought that it was just a watch.

The Bible tells us that God created a magnificent world. Unfortunately, most people take life and this world for granted. But, obviously, as you would see from reading His book, He's a very kind, caring Creator Who created a world that has even more than 14-karat gold, more than seventeen kinds of jewels, contains a built-in calendar, and provides us with perfect built-in timepieces that never need fixing. He wants us to appreciate all of the wonderful things He put here. He wants us to know that the more we find out about the capabilities of our world, the more we will see that everything in it and everything that happens here is for the good. We just have to look.

Point number two: Suppose instead of giving you a watch, I gave you a "solarcast" with all of the latest features including buttons, dials, and gadgets, completely upgradable with a lifetime guarantee. What would you do with it? Probably nothing, because nobody knows what a "solarcast" is. But let's say it came with a complete set of instructions. After you read them, study them and decipher them, you will find that when used properly, your gift will bring you all of the joys of this world. Chances are you would want to take a look.

God gave us each a life, but few of us know how to use it properly, so we just drift along hoping to catch some wisps of pleasure. But wouldn't that be a cruel irony – a God Who gives us a gift that we don't know how to use? So He gave us an instruction book, a guideline for successful living, and it's called the Bible. It teaches us how to push the right buttons and operate all of the advanced features. But it takes work. His guarantee? A lifetime of happiness.

Are we here in this world to achieve perfection of character? To enjoy the true pleasures of life? To give thanks and devote ourselves to the One Who gave everything to us? All of the above. The Bible is the manual that shows us how to succeed. We can try to achieve this on our own, or when all else fails, we can read the instructions.

The
Next
Step

STEPPING UP
TO THE PLATE

"Mr. Crawford, this is National City Bank and I'm calling about that missed payment on your mortgage."

"Mr. Crawford, this is the nurse from your son's school. He took a little flop during recess today. You might want to take him to your family doctor. I'm sure he'll be ok."

"Roger, don't forget we're having dinner with my parents tonight."

"Crawford! Come in to my office; there's something we need to discuss."

Did you ever feel that you were on a treadmill going nowhere? It's a very common feeling. In today's society with all of the pressures to succeed in business, family life and the social scene, it's very easy to get caught up in this everyday world and say, "What's it all about? Why am I here?"

How would you go about finding out the answer? Let's first see what some other people think about it.

About ten years ago, *Newsweek* magazine conducted a survey of approximately 10,000 American high school kids and asked them what would be the most awesome experience they could imagine. A lot of the boys immediately responded, "Five minutes one-on-one with Michael Jordan." Many of the girls said, "Wow! I'd love to meet the cast of 'Titanic'." But the majority of them said that the most amazing experience they could think of would be to meet God.

So let's imagine you come home from work one day and you see this brilliant light shining from your living room window. You unlock the door and you hear a deep voice say, "Roger, take off your shoes from upon your feet, for the ground upon which you are standing is holy ground."

And there He is – you sense God, in your own living room.

What do you think you would say?

Some people would be content to find out who was going to win this year's Super Bowl, or what's tonight's winning lottery number, or the best pick in the stock market. What do you think *you* would ask Him? I know what I would ask.

I would say, after my knees stopped shaking, "Dearest God, what is my purpose in life? Why have You put me here?"

Sounds like a doozy of a question, right? Let's say He told me something crazy like, "You are here to coach Little League."

What? I don't even like baseball! I don't even know how to throw a ball. I always thought the cleanup batter was the guy who dusted off home plate. What did He mean by that?

Whether I understood it or not, if I believed that this was my purpose in life, I would try to be the best darned Little League coach in the universe. And every time I taught a child how to hit a ball or slide into second base, I would take great pride in knowing that I was fulfilling my role in this world.

And then suppose, one day, the governor calls me up and tells me he wants me to coach the State's Special Olympics Baseball

Team. And there I am, building up the pride and self-respect of twenty disabled youngsters who might never have had the chance to experience the thrill of hitting a home run or catching a fly ball if it weren't for me. I then might better understand that my purpose in life was not just baseball, but to bring joy and happiness to others through the use of my God-given talents.

But most of us will never meet God face to face. Does that mean we can never discover our purpose and goal? Or perhaps there is no such thing anyway. Maybe we are only here as accidents of nature with no more purpose in life than an amoeba.

Does that make sense, though? Look at the people around you. Everyone is trying in his own way to make a mark on the world. Whether it's by having their name inscribed on the cornerstone of a building, or trying to find the cure for a disease or simply naming their grandchildren after them, most people want to leave something to posterity. Instinctively we know that there is a deeper meaning to life than mere existence.

So how does one find meaning?

Unfortunately, God doesn't make house calls. But the path to finding meaning in life can begin in your own living room. It's a multi-step process. The first step is one that people think about doing, but usually never do. It is, simply, to write out a list of things that are important to you in life. (A good hot cup of coffee to get you going in the morning may be important and pleasant, but it's not one of those life-goal things we're talking about.) It should be things like:

> ‣ A good marriage

> ‣ Success in business (to be defined by you either as making a lot of money, getting a lot of honor, offering the best product, doing business honestly, etc.)

> ‣ A close circle of trusted friends

> ‣ The nicest house on the block

> ‣ Helping the underprivileged

> ‣ Saving whales

- Becoming famous

- Looking good, always

- Raising a good family (once again to be defined by you as loving, caring, attractive, value-based, outgoing, fun-loving, religious, etc.)

- Protecting the world from the spread of communism, fundamentalism, Democrats/Republicans, disease, poverty and hunger.

Once you've taken the first step, the second step is even more critical. Review your list objectively and decide which of the above items you are willing to die for.

- Would you be willing to risk a heart attack to get that next order from Walmart?

- Would you dive into the ocean to save a whale? What about saving your child?

- Would you join the US Army to fight an evil enemy?

- Would you be ready to kill yourself if the living room furniture doesn't match the rug?

Chances are, when you get through crossing out, you will have two major items left on your list: family and values. Whether these values relate to how you conduct your life in business, in society, or in the privacy of your own home, some of them are truly worth dying for.

Now that you have a focus, the most important step is to *live* for what's important. Finding meaning in life is important, but taking action and accomplishing your goal is what *gives* meaning to life, giving you unparalleled power and pleasure. Even the mundane tasks of this everyday world become enriching.

If you are a housewife raising young children, then every time you do the laundry, cook a meal or help with homework, you are fulfilling your life's goal.

If your goal is to teach values, then every time you return the extra change to the cashier, or admit when you are wrong, or refrain from gossiping about another person, you are setting an example for others to follow.

If your goal is to help others, then every time you use your particular talents you are making the world a better place – which is what you acknowledged is your purpose for being here in the first place! This can take the form of philanthropy, if you are rich; creating beautiful paintings, if you're artistic; teaching, if you're smart; or coaching a baseball team – in the unlikely event that God happens to show up in your living room one day and tells you to.

I NOW PRONOUNCE YOU...

Richie and Ellen had been dating for over a year. He was a successful real estate developer and she was a designer at one of the fashion houses on New York's famous Seventh Avenue. They did everything together from picnicking, tennis, and shopping, to helping the sick and feeding the homeless on Thanksgiving.

As their lives grew together, it came time for Richie to pop the question.

He did, and she said yes. They began that joyous, hectic period of planning their wedding and looking for a place to live. Time flew by as the day of their wedding quickly approached.

Two weeks before that blessed day, Richie told Ellen it was time to have a very serious talk. Ellen assumed that this was just one more instance of Richie checking all the fine details.

She was right. They met that night after work at their usual table at the local Starbucks Coffee Shop. Richie began: "Ellen, you know I've been fortunate over the last few years to put together quite a big nest egg from all of the real estate deals I've made and I – I just want to be sure that we have a clear understanding of what would happen to all of it in case, you know, just in case things didn't work out between us."

"I'm not exactly sure what you're saying, Richie. You know you've always kept that side of your life to yourself and I have no intention of butting in now."

Richie gave a sigh of relief. "Well, good, good. But I'm really talking about something different."

At this point he pulled out a single sheet of paper. "You see, I've drawn up sort of a prenuptial agreement, in case, I mean like, whatever, you know."

"Sure, I understand. Let me see it."

At first, Ellen was impressed with the way Richie was handling this. There they were having this "very serious talk," just the two of them. No lawyers, no financial advisers. Richie had even done all of the typing himself. "Probably because he loves me so much and trusts me," she thought.

As she started reading, she became a little perturbed by all of the "whereas" clauses, but she just assumed that was the way that pre-nups were written. It read like this:

> **Wh**ereas we've known each other for a long time, and
>
> **Wh**ereas we plan on getting married, and
>
> **Wh**ereas most of the wealth coming into the marriage is really mine, therefore it is understood that:
>
> ▶ 1. I will provide for your well-being including the fun things like exotic vacations, a new car every two or three years, a house of our own and maybe even a vacation home as long as we're able to afford them.

▶ 2. You'll take care of the house stuff and bringing up our kids.

▶ 3. We'll make important decisions together – like where to live, what school to send our kids to and how long you can continue to work.

▶ 4. In case we break up, you get to keep only our principal residence, one car and the kids (unless I find out that you wronged me, in which case I will fight you tooth and nail to get everything back).

▶ 5. In the event of my death, the insurance money and all of my assets go 50% to you and 50% to our kids (unless you were the one who killed me; only kidding, Ellen, ha ha).

▶ 6. In case of divorce, everything in my business, now or in the future, is mine.

Signed in agreement this day _____

by both parties

_____ and _____

Ellen took a sip of her coffee.

She read it through again.

Something was missing. It should have been in the "where-as's," but it wasn't there. She looked at Richie and asked, "Where does it say that you love me?"

Richie laughed and said, "I'll put a little heart over the "i" in my signature."

"No, really, Richie. I understand that this is business, but we're talking about marriage. You know I don't care about your money. We've never even discussed your business affairs. I'm marrying you, Richie, the man I love. I wouldn't want your possessions, especially if I didn't have you."

Richie stared into his cup of cappuccino. "I don't understand what your problem is, Ellen. Of course I plan on staying with you forever, but you know, things can happen. But while we're togeth-er, think of all the great things we can do. We can go places; we can buy things. I can surprise you with jewelry or tickets to a show. It'll be fun."

"But what about you? If I don't have a part of you, then all I'm doing is taking, not sharing. That's not marriage."

"I'm giving you part of everything I own, isn't that enough?"

"No," she whispered almost inaudibly.

Richie did not reply.

After several painful moments, Ellen stood up to leave. As she raised her hand to wipe the tears from her eyes, she accidentally spilled her coffee all over the agreement.

A few days later, the wedding was called off. Fortunately for Richie, he got to keep all of his stuff.

Funny thing about us – human beings want things, we like to get them, but we hate to just take them. We like to feel that we've earned them, unless they come from someone we love and who loves us back. For with that love, taking is also giving.

However, some things have such high price tags on them that we can never really pay for them in the normal sense of the word. Look at some of the stuff we get without even asking:

Rain, fruit, trees, snow, lightning, freon, air, water, light, teeth, food, kidneys, antibodies, clothing, bodies, language, memory, forgetfulness, wisdom, herbal teas, life, and even death, the passport to immortality.

These things, which all of the money in the world cannot pay for, are coming to us free of charge from the Ultimate Giver. His riches far exceed the wealth of all of the people who ever lived or will live. Through Him we all can share in everything. And since everything belongs to and is part of Him, He is actually giving of Himself.

He's looking for each one of us to be His lifelong partner, to share in His being. But it takes reciprocal love. Are you up to the task? If not, then you're just a taker and you can never get true pleasure from all of His bounty. If yes, then by the power vested in me, I now pronounce you...

AUNT SOPHIE

This is a story about appreciation. It's a story about Aunt Sophie. Everybody has an Aunt Sophie, right? Or maybe an Aunt Gladys or an Aunt Florence? Actually, it's about all three of them.

You're planning a wedding. It's going to be a gala event for your one and only daughter and it's going to be great. You're planning it down to the last detail – food, flowers, music, invitations, seating arrangements, the bridesmaids' gowns, the tablecloths, the works. You want it to be perfect.

Aunt Sophie is your favorite aunt and you know that she's definitely going to come. A long time ago she told you that she loves to have some herbal tea with her dessert; it settles her stomach after all that rich food. So you make sure that there's going to be herbal tea at the dessert table.

Aunt Gladys is also coming, but she never likes anything. It seems that she's always going through life complaining about something. So there's nothing that you can do that's going to make this wedding any more or less enjoyable for Aunt Gladys.

It's the night of the wedding and everything is beautiful. The bride, the hall, the flowers – even your husband looks presentable for once.

The ceremony is over. You cried, the in-laws cried, the rabbi cried. The dinner is served to perfection. The music is wonderful. After the cake-cutting ceremony, it's time for dessert. Sure enough, on the table there's a full display of herbal teas. Aunt Sophie goes over to the table, takes her cup of tea, takes a little chocolate mousse, and is in heaven.

She comes over to you afterwards and says, "Susie, I can't believe you went to all this trouble just for me." You tell her, "Really, Aunt Sophie, it was my pleasure. It was no trouble at all."

How does Aunt Sophie feel? Like a million bucks, because you did something especially for her.

What about Aunt Gladys? "Herbal, shmerbal, what do I care? Give me some coffee. I'm gonna be up all night anyway from that chicken; it was so greasy, who could eat it?"

Here you went through all the trouble of making a picture-perfect evening and she was too busy complaining to enjoy it.

Now, of course, let's not forget Aunt Florence. Aunt Florence has two choices. Number one, she can drink tea or she can drink coffee. But she has a bigger choice to make. You see, she can also choose whether to look at the evening as if you did everything for her, or that it all just happened to be there for all of the guests to enjoy.

What difference would it make? Even if you never thought about Auntie Florence and you never knew that she loved herbal tea, imagine how much better *she* would feel thinking that you did it all for her! She would feel so special, just like Aunt Sophie. Is she fooling herself? Perhaps, but in the end, she got so much more pleasure out of a simple cup of tea, thinking that it was put there especially for her.

Even if you don't accept anything that's been presented in this book, even if you still think it's all nonsense and everything only happens by accident – when you look around at the things you have, how much more could you enjoy them if you felt that it was done only for your benefit? That everything that you have and everything that happens to you are only for your individual needs. In fact, Judaism tells you that you are *supposed* to look at the world as if it were *all* created just for you!

Doesn't everything now become so much more special? Doesn't it make *you* more special – to know that all of it was placed in this world just for you? And if everything was put here intentionally for you, Someone must have placed it there.

When you first put on a new pair of glasses or you put in your contacts for the first time, the whole world looked different, as though you've never seen it before. It's clear. It's perfect. What if I put on your glasses? Things wouldn't look right; everything would be out of focus. Because that prescription is designed specifically for you and my prescription is designed perfectly for me.

The world works the same way. Everything is provided for your individual benefit. It suits you to a tea (Aunt Sophie's brand). Recognize it and appreciate it.

So now we've arrived at the final question. What should you do about what you've just learned? How do you cash in and get the most out of life?

Please turn the page.

THE REWARD

f you have come to the conclusion that "The Next Step" is gratitude, then you are already halfway there.

This process begins by learning to say "thank you." When something happens to you and it goes your way, and it could have just as easily gone the other way, just take a moment and say "thank you."

I'll give you an example. Every day at work, I eat a little container of yogurt. I figure if I'm going to live to 120, it's going to take a lot of yogurt. Invariably, at least once a week, I drip some of it off the side of the spoon. When I look down and I see that it fell on my desk or on my shirt, and not on my $45 tie, I say thank you: first for not ruining my tie, and secondly for not putting me through the test of seeing how I would react if it did fall on my tie. (I'm very sensitive about my ties.)

I'll give you a bigger example:

Imagine you received a notice to serve on Grand Jury duty in New York – a case involving corruption in the city government. The judge tells you that, if selected, you would have the privilege of serving in his court for two to three days per week for the next six months, with a possible extension of another three months. You try everything you can to get out of it, but nothing works.

They need thirty people to serve on the jury and there are about 200 people who have been summoned to appear. At first glance, you think that your odds are pretty good. Then the bailiff says, if anyone works for the government or has a spouse who works for the government, or if you're a teacher or meet any of a number of other exemptions, you can be excused. A hundred people get up, turn around, and march out of the room. Well, so much for playing the odds.

Next, they explain the benefits: $15 a day, plus $2.50 for transportation. Some days you may get out at three o'clock. You can't talk to anyone about the case for a year.

And now they ask for volunteers. To your great amazement (and relief), eighteen people volunteer. (Did you ever imagine what these people do with themselves when they don't have jury duty?)

Now they still have to draft twelve more jurors. They take the names of all of the remaining people, about 70 of you, and they put them into one of those rotating drums. Now, even if you've never won the lottery before, it appears that your luck is about to change.

One by one, they start drawing names out of the hopper. After each name, the person goes and sits with the other jurors. After every name they go back to the juror section and recount the number of people that are sitting there, just to make sure that no one escaped.

This process takes about 30 to 40 minutes. By this time, your heart is pounding, you're sweating, and you're sitting at the edge of your chair as though you're awaiting a death sentence.

Finally, it comes down to the last slot. Your heart is in your mouth and you're waiting for them to call your name. The bailiff reaches in, gets the slip of paper, holds it up and says: "Hawthorne Thatcheray."

You jump out of your seat and the first words that come out of your mouth are: "Thank God!" (I'm assuming here that your name is not Hawthorne Thatcheray.) You hand in your juror's slip and run out of that room as fast as your legs can carry you.

It's a lot bigger, a lot more emotional, but still, a simple thank you. That's the most basic way: when something good happens, just say thank you.

There's a second, higher level. When a person recognizes that all that he has comes from God, that everything good that happens to him is because of God, then it's time to say, "What can I give back to You, dear God, for all the good that You have given me?"

At a family gathering, for example, when you look around the dining room table and you see your family, your children, your spouse, how everyone is dressed so beautifully, that you can afford to have a home, a car, delicious food, that everyone is healthy, that everyone talks to one another, that you appreciate what it means to be a good person, that you live in freedom in the greatest country in the history of the world, that you are free to practice religion without persecution, that you weren't born into poverty or oppression. When you can appreciate all of these wonderful things and more, then it's time to say, "Creator of the Universe, how can I ever repay You for all of the good You've given me?"

When you can say that and mean it, you have achieved the second level of saying thank you. Easy to say, not so easy to achieve.

Finally, there's a third level. This is the point where you say, "It's You, God. Not only have You given me everything, but You've given me life. You breathed a part of Yourself into me and made me what I am today. You have nurtured me, provided for me, rewarded me and punished me. You've taught me values. You've given the world a guidebook to show us all how to achieve the maximum pleasure out of life. You are more than a parent to me.

You are my very essence. What I have, what I am, is only because of You. And for all of that, I love You."

When you can look up to heaven and say, "I love You, God – with all of my heart and all of my soul and all of my might," then you have achieved greatness. The highest level of attachment to God, the ultimate pleasure in this world, is to love Him.

To many people this sounds very odd. They've never thought of the idea of loving God, but it is said twice a day in the Hebrew prayer of *Shema*. One of first words of the prayer, "*Ve'ahavta*," is in fact a commandment: it is to love God.

It's not as hard as it sounds. When one contemplates the exalted position of the King of Kings and how small we are compared to the entire universe, the fact that we warrant any of His attention at all should be enough to overwhelm us with emotions of love and gratitude.

It's like the story of a child who was born into a prison belonging to a king. For whatever reason, the king ordered one of his royal officers to take care of him and provide everything he needed for his well-being. The child only knows the prison and its contents.

So every day the officer brings the child food, drinks and clothing. One day, when the child is finally old enough to understand, the officer tells him that, in fact, he is a servant to the king and that the prison and all it contains belongs to the king. The child is told that he therefore has an obligation to thank the king.

The child immediately replies, "Praise to the king who has accepted me as his servant and has singled me out for all of his bounty and favored me with special attention. I am forever grateful."

The officer, who obviously knows that the king owns a lot more than just the prison, tells him, "The king's royal domain far exceeds the confines of this prison. You're not his only servant. In fact, he has thousands of them, and the kindnesses he shows to you are insignificant compared to the benefits he bestows on others."

Now, finally, the child has some understanding of the king's powers, of the fact that he is a benefactor to everyone in the kingdom, and that the exalted state of the king far exceeds his own lowly position.

In many ways, we are like that child in the prison. We can only see a small portion of all that God does for the world. When we try to thank Him, words alone can't express our gratitude because we can't fully appreciate the magnitude of kindnesses that we receive from Him every instant of every day.

How many times do we go against God's wishes? How many times do we do things we shouldn't, or don't do the things we should? Yet God continues to give to us and to love us, regardless of how many times we reject Him or ignore Him. God is the benevolent and kind Master that continues to feed us and clothe us, no matter how many times we rebel. His love and His bounty are limitless.

And what is it that God asks of us in return? Just to love Him and fear Him – the way a child feels toward his parents – and to emulate Him by doing acts of kindness to others. When we do, we are in reality saying, "Father in Heaven, I want to be like You." What greater "thank you" can a child give to a parent than wanting to walk in his footsteps?

Can we ever know enough about God to become like Him – God Who is infinite and unknowable? We're fortunate in that we have an insight into the mind of God called the Bible. By reading, studying and following its precepts we are taking the most precious gift ever given to mankind and elevating it to the highest plateau.

Rabbi Avigdor Miller loved to say, "When you get out of the train in Manhattan in the morning – as you're walking down the street to your office – if you stop and say, "I love You, God," you are unique in all of New York: you have achieved greatness."

There are just three simple steps to achieving the maximum pleasure that this world has to offer:

Recognize that there is a God, the Creator of the universe, Who is all-knowing, all-powerful, kind, merciful, loving, infinitely patient and awesome (not cool, awesome).

Appreciate everything that He does for you, from curing a headache to providing you with a magnificent universe to live in.

And finally, with all your heart and all your soul and all your might, just say, "thank you."

Thank you.